MUSTARD
Seed

A STORY OF FAITH.
A JOURNEY OF HEALING.
A MESSAGE OF HOPE.

EILEEN ALBRECHT

ISBN 978-1-64416-748-9 (paperback)
ISBN 978-1-64416-749-6 (digital)

Christian Faith Publishing, Inc.
832 Park Avenue
Meadville, PA 16335
www.christianfaithpublishing.com

Cover art created by Maureen O'keefe-Strang, sm2strang@gmail.com

Printed in the United States of America

In loving memory of editor
Joann Catherine "Cathy" Adams,
1949–2016

ACKNOWLEDGMENTS

I wrote this book in thanksgiving to God for the gift of life. I dedicate it to my mother, Ellen Mary (Patch) Wickenheiser, in gratitude for the faith she inspired in me. I am forever grateful to my father, Earl August Wickenheiser, for his steadfast love, discipline, and faithful provision; and to both for the gift of family.

Thanks to my own children Rochelle, Leah, Claire, and Ethan, the greatest blessings I have ever received; thank you for helping me to grow! Also, to David Albrecht, my husband, my knight in shining armor, whose amazing love has saved me from myself by inspiring me to heal. Special thanks to my family and family of friends in my community's churches who helped sustain us during my son's illness and who continue to bless our lives with their friendship and prayers.

> "May the LORD, the God of your ancestors, increase you a thousand times and bless you as He has promised!" (Deuteronomy 1:11, NIV).

"If you have faith as small as a mustard seed, you can say to this mountain, 'Move from here to there,' and it will move. Nothing will be impossible for you."
—Matthew 17:20b (NIV)

CONTENTS

FOREWORD

"The fruit of the Spirit is love, joy,
peace, patience, kindness, generosity, faithfulness, gentleness, self-con-
trol. Against such there is no law."
—Galatians 5:22–23 (NABRE)

In this groundbreaking classic linking prayer and health,
the author shares evidence connecting prayer, healing, and
medicine. Using real-life examples and personal anecdotes,
she proves how prayer can be as valid a healing tool as
drugs or surgery. Her most challenging circumstances were
those about which she could do absolutely nothing. She
did everything possible that she knew to do and then continued doing her best to go about her daily routine, while
courageously awaiting an uncertain outcome. To relieve
the burden of this period, she put one foot in front of the
other, acting as if things would turn out as she hoped. She
used the time to strengthen her trust in God, remembering
that He alone can provide endurance and calm strength
needed for those long intervals of uncertainty that cannot
be escaped.

As a friend and as a writer, Eileen is innocently trusting, generous, loving, and expressive. Eileen's writing is chatty, deep, confident, and self-deprecating, which make her work engaging and accessible. A captivating, intelligent, deeply entertaining memoir, her account of her life is beautiful and honest. A fast-paced spiritual memoir, it is also a journey filled with delightful metaphor, excellent mini profiles, divine experience, and serious soul searching. Eileen is a likeable pilgrim on a hero's journey.

Healthcare practitioners and patients alike will benefit from reading this practical, creative book. It is a wonderful reminder of how important it is to integrate all we know about getting well. It offers a genuine program embracing the emotional, physical, psychological, and spiritual aspects of healing. It is a timely book that speaks to the mind and the heart simultaneously. It is sure to whet our already burgeoning appetite for information on functional medicine.

Eileen's book has provided her a precious opportunity to recount and bravely share a very personal healing journey. It is a great joy to behold unselfish love, where there is nothing expected in return, in truth—a foretaste of heaven. Eileen's struggles reflect a perfect faith, responding to trials in a way that lifted her absolutely above her fears. As her faith grew, so did her inner security, knowing that God was always with her, providing, protecting, and caring every step of the way. I believe that *Mustard Seed* will be of great value to those wishing to understand and apply holistic concepts of health to real-life challenges, including a crisis of faith.

Dr. Joseph Cannizzaro, MD, has been practicing in Central Florida for over thirty years and provides the Orlando area with its only functional-integrative pediatric practice. Dr. Cannizzaro is certified by ABIHM, the American Board of Integrative Holistic Medicine. As a classically trained primary care physician who practices functional medicine, Dr. Cannizzaro believes that integrative medicine can bring conventional and complementary healing modalities together, creating a highly personalized and high-touch healing environment. Known for his genuine compassion, Dr. Cannizzaro is dedicated to providing children and their families with healthier, happier, and longer lives. (http://mycipc.com/dr-cannizzaro/)

THROUGH THE EYES OF ETHAN'S SISTER

"(We) He shall not fear an ill report; his
heart is steadfast, trusting the LORD."
—Psalm 112:7 (NABRE)

Leah Rae
April 2, 1997

I was only fourteen years old at the time, but I clearly remember the image of her face as she walked toward us, as if it had been burned into the back of my eyes. That summer was one of the hottest I could recall. Everything I looked at seemed to have steam rising from its surface. The heat made me grateful to be inside in the air-conditioning even if I happened to be at the doctor's office.

My little three-year-old brother Ethan and I were dispensed to the car as Ethan's doctor took my mother, Eileen, aside to talk. Ethan reached for her in protest, so I scooped him up and headed outside. He was dressed in his usual white undershirt, the kind with snaps between the legs, his soft limbs exposed and shaggy Beatle-esque hair damp with sweat. We waited in the van with the windows down while the vents attempted to produce cool air at a tolerable temperature.

Ethan had always been impatient, and I had to reassure him multiple times that Mom would be right out, while my own patience was melting away. I helped buckle him into his car seat, closed the windows, and began searching the radio for something we could sing along to. As I sat staring at the office door, it created a growing sense of anxiety within me. I thought about all the sicknesses that had passed through and that would continue to come and go through that door. I turned to look at the hospital that lay a parking lot's distance behind us, and I wondered how awful it must be for the people inside. Before I could lose myself in daydreaming, the movement of the burgundy door of the doctor's office brought my attention to Mom.

I can't remember if we had gone to the doctor's office because Ethan had a fever or if it was some other complaint. However, despite the fact that I didn't know the reason, we went there that day, I will never forget why our mother looked the way she did as we left.

Our mother is a beautiful woman, yet the face she wore as she moved toward the van made me wish I had been born blind. Her look was filled with the dread of a coming war. It would be the kind of war we both had experienced in the past and one that had made casualties of members of our beloved family.

When she got into the car, I quickly shut off the radio (she never did care for channel surfing). I could see the tears forming in her eyes. Likely, they had been shoved back only moments ago, although pessimism had a moment to set in and they refused to submit to composure.

As we slowly pulled out of the parking lot, I summoned enough courage to talk. I knew why she was crying without asking, but conversation sometimes has a way of alleviating anxiety. I felt my throat closing as I forced the words out of my mouth, "What did the doctor say?" Her reply was slow and separated by conscious breaths, "I have to take Ethan to Ann Arbor." I knew then that our lives were changed. He could not go to the hospital that was only feet away. He had to go where there were doctors who specialized in what he needed. Without any test results, we trusted that the doctor knew Ethan needed to go to Children's Hospital and that is where we would take him.

On the drive home, I listened as my mom made phone call after phone call asking for prayer and letting the people who loved us know that Ethan was not well. The rush of the cold air blowing on my face and the desperate tone in my mother's voice evoked such a sense of fear that I felt I only had to blink and everything I loved would be lost. I pushed myself into the high back of the bucket seat and tried to conceal my tears from Ethan. The burning sensation in my throat grew as I looked to the window for distraction. Her voice finally breaking, Mom handed me the phone asking me to call Aunt Chris and tell her to go immediately to our house. We rode in silence the remaining few minutes until we reached home.

Aunt Chris arrived at our house within minutes to go to the hospital with Mom and Ethan. She would return that night to tell Rochelle, Claire, and me that our little brother had cancer. At that moment, I would wish for the first time, of many times, that it was me instead of him.

"Say to the fearful of heart:
Be strong, do not fear!
Here is your God,
He comes with vindication;
With divine recompense
He comes to save you."
—Isaiah 35:4 (NABRE)

MUSTARD SEED

Once I heard a story, from who I don't remember
But I knew I'd heard this Name before,
When I was very small, I'm sure.
And who can say how it might have been,
Had I kept on listening,
Instead of searching all about for a feel-
ing I thought I couldn't live without.
So I started on a long, dark, rocky road alone.
And the scars are deep for the wounds I keep
and that keep me from coming home.
Then I recall, when I was small,
There was a place that I could go and leave it all.
At the feet of Jesus, and if He'll still
have me, I want to come home.
As I say these words, I feel the burden being lifted.
And silently I thank the one who sowed
the seed while I was young.
And what I went without, I found
within those simple stories;
A Shepherd and His straying sheep, a prod-
igal son and a mustard seed.

I recall, when I was small,
There was a place that I could go and leave it all.
At the feet of Jesus, and if He'll still
have me, I want to come home.
Home, Jesus. I want to come home to You.
I want to come home. Mercy, Jesus. I
want to come home to You.
Once I heard a story, from who I don't remember.
But silently I thank the one, who sowed
the seed while I was young.
(*Song by Eileen*)

INTRODUCTION

With perfect hindsight, I now see that what I thought I had "stumbled into" on my quest for inner healing was nothing more than my understanding catching up with the plan God had for me all along. It began when I discovered a process of prayer practiced at a local nondenominational church in my hometown in Michigan. It was a prayer revealed to a discouraged Southern Baptist minister named Dr. Ed Smith, who was seeking God's help to relieve the suffering of the abused women and others he was working with in his counseling ministry and pastoral care.

This prayer was originally and aptly named to mean "God's Light." With Transformation Prayer Ministry (TPM), the healing light of Jesus Christ who is the Way, the Truth, and the Life (John 14:6) is being invited into the origin of the hurt and pain we are suffering and consistently reveals what we believe about what we have experienced. The beliefs that keep us bound to the pain are exposed and then the deeper Truth of Christ sets us free.

"So if the Son sets you free, you will
be free indeed" (John 8:36, NIV).

Transformation Prayer Ministry (www.transformation prayer.org) remains a helpful tool for those seeking relief from emotional pain. Dr. Ed Smith observes, "It is not the memory that needs to be healed, it is what we continue to believe about what happened that prolongs the pain." As a result, the Fruit of the Spirit becomes evident in the lives of those who experience this prayer (Gal. 5:22–23).

Of course, we encounter God in many ways, and He heals as He wills. It seems for many like me though, that there are certain emotions that act more like a harsh taskmaster rather than simply a thermometer gauging a thought pattern. It was in that state that I found a Transformation Prayer Ministry counselor. Through our prayer, I began to understand that the parts of me that I could not control and that had the potential to lead me to sin were expressions of and a *distraction from* my emotional pain.

I had a lot of practice controlling my thoughts and reactions in the past, but it took a tremendous amount of effort. I learned that the strong negative emotions rising again and again were indicators that I held a negative belief that was driving my reaction. It's much like an annoying security warning that pops up on my computer to indicate something is wrong. It prevents me from going any further until I investigate the problem. After experiencing this prayer, I began to choose to view those triggers as a help instead of an annoyance.

In fact, that was the purpose of these emotions. Without understanding the trigger (or negative belief) that caused me to react in an adverse way, I would continue to exert enormous energy trying to "be good" or suffer hours of guilt when I would inevitably "lose it." Figuratively, if I were on my imaginary prayer computer and were to type (or name) the emotion I was feeling into the "search box," it would lead me to a file that contains a memory of when I first formed the strong belief that was now negatively influencing me.

Jesus is eager to heal our wounds and wants us to live free from all fear. In His presence, we can find peace in our circumstances. With the help of TPM, I began experiencing freedom in the place where I first formed hindering beliefs, and it effortlessly changed how I viewed my present situation—the key word being "effortlessly." The prayer results in a true change of heart.

> "A new heart also will I give you, and
> a new spirit will I put within you; and I
> will take away the stony heart out of your
> flesh, and I will give you a heart of flesh"
> (Ezek. 36:26, KJV).

I am still in awe of the relief that TPM has brought me. I had been diligently seeking the Lord's healing as I searched for purpose and meaning, especially in suffering, when I came across the brochure for TPM. I didn't like the way I felt or how I was handling life and I needed God's peace. With TPM, it was as if I was handed a special-looking glass that enabled me to observe my life in a way I could never have grasped before. I have had the privilege of looking at my past experiences through the lens of Love, through the eyes of the One who desired for me to be here and to be whole. He is the one who can bring good out of everything, even those things that I perceive as not being good.

Since I have experienced God's presence in my prayer, I am now better able to understand and accept His will as my life unfolds. It has changed how I view my journey of faith. It has helped give me greater understanding of the Father's love. I came to understand in a real way how my sin separates me from God but not because it changes His view of me—as His love is perfect, and He will never love me more than He already does. However, now I desire a heart where He is pleased to dwell.

I am rediscovering God's promise, "I am come that they might have life, and that they might have it more abundantly" (John 10:10b, KJV). God did not intend for me to dwell in my past mistakes and sin but instead to learn from them, receive His forgiveness, and enjoy new life. It is my purpose in turn, to shine God's light through the telling of my story. I want to share the journey of how I began to see His presence and purpose working itself out in my life—the joys, mistakes, sufferings, and transformation.

I have begun to see my life as a tapestry that the Master's skillful hand weaves into a work of priceless art. Like a thread pulled from beneath a loom, I somehow emerge on top, no longer tangled below where the chaotic ends hang. Elevated, I can see how strand by painstaking strand, a brilliant landscape was being created with deliberate precision. The good and the bad were being woven together as if two threads were entwined in a single string. From here, I can see that no stitch was a mistake. The process was no accident.

This is my story, though each of us has one that could be told differently by everyone who knows us. Our stories even change over time. Memories change as we change, and we begin to view them with an insight, maturity, wisdom, and understanding that we did not have at the time of our experiences.

Can you imagine how life would look if we took the time to listen and understand each other's story or even reflected on the importance of our own? Would we see the threads of the Master's handiwork woven in the consequential and mundane patterns of our life? Could we be more open and truthful with each other if we truly believed that there was a higher purpose to each encounter? What is it that makes us afraid of judgment, criticism, and rejection? Will understanding be sacrificed for external appearances if we are afraid to acknowledge emotions that arise and make us feel uncomfortable?

Joyce Meyers, one of the world's leading practical Bible teachers, has mentored me through her books and recordings for many years. She constantly reminds her readers to apply God's word to our ordinary daily lives. She relates that the Bible assures us the truth will set you free (John 8:31–32). She encourages us to be honest with others about what is going on inside and to allow the Holy Spirit to use our experiences. As she says, she is a witness that with God's help our mess becomes our message, our test becomes our testimony.

After repeatedly hearing her say this, I began to question how fear might be preventing me from sharing what God was doing in my life. I wondered what kind of changes would have occurred earlier in my life if I had the wisdom to listen with my heart and if I had recognized the prompting of the Holy Spirit when I suspected God was trying to get my attention. Who might I have helped if I had more readily shared what I was learning with those who crossed my path? Could my story contain a key to help free others?

I pray now in the retelling of my story. Perhaps I will see myself differently if I peer through the glass of the Maker, the One who chisels away at the stony places, assured of a precious diamond beneath. I pray to grasp and accept that He alone knew when it was necessary to apply pressure for the job to be accomplished. I trust that the people and circumstances He brought into my life, whether welcome or not, were used as His tools to accomplish His purpose. Pressure exerted effectively eliminates flaws making the stone more valuable. It releases a faceted gem for my good and ultimately to reflect His love to others.

I noticed a new excitement for life when I began actively looking for and acknowledging God's presence in life. I began asking for wisdom, for His take on what was happening day to day, from my noticing a sudden change in my mood, experiencing an unforeseen event, to having an unexpected conversation. Expectantly keeping one ear open to His voice, when painful memories came forward, I would sense a subtle answer to the simple TPM prayer that I learned to pray. I asked, "Lord, what do *You* want me to know about this?" In response, I began to recognize His answer as having the same tone that I heard when I read the Scriptures.

I realized God cared about every aspect of my life, and He was able to guide my reactions and actions if I were willing to let Him. I also began to observe the results in my interactions with others. I had heard that the effect you have on others is the most valuable currency there is, and I wondered what portion of my encounters gave glory to God for what He purchased for me.

I learned that whether I was conscious of it or not at the time, my motives were deeply intentioned in my beliefs. My beliefs could also influence the way I acted and reacted to others depending on what I learned from my past experiences. It convinced me of the importance of bringing Jesus, Light of God's Truth, into the memories that were still causing me pain. The connection between the experience and my belief was so strong that I was literally bound unless my beliefs were rebuilt on the foundation of God's freeing truth. Asking God for deeper truth about hurts and fears from past traumatic experiences results in tremendous relief.

> "Send out your light and your truth;
> let them lead me; let them bring me to
> your holy hill and to your dwelling!"
> (Ps. 43:3, ESV).

The greatest storytellers are those whose stories resonate deeply within us. The emotions they invoke cause us to empathize, give us a glimpse of another's perspective, or perhaps even challenge us to consider where our beliefs originally came from. They can have the power to inspire us to seek healing and motivate us to grow or, if need be, to change. Jesus accomplished this in His use of parables.

When we share how God is working in our life, He can continue to bring His light to a darkening world.

> "So will My word be which goes forth from My mouth; It will not return to Me empty, without accomplishing what I desire, and without succeeding in the matter for which I sent it" (Isa. 55:11, NASB).

I collected my story in volumes of journals for many years. I never expected to share them but hoped that they would help me understand the changes I experienced when returning to the Faith as I further sought to surrender my life to the Lord. It would be easier to write this now if I still had those journals. Although I had documented the joys, tears, and lessons on my journey to discovering the love of God, my journals have long been laid to rest in the ashes of my backyard fire pit. They were burned there years ago in desperation the night my son's doctor called, three years into our battle with his leukemia. I was told Ethan, at the tender age of six, had developed a secondary cancer from the chemotherapy and radiation.

Wearily, I hung up the phone having been told by the doctor to prepare myself for what was to come next. Alone, I stumbled out into the darkness, my journals in hand. Creating a teepee of small kindling, I ignited each page as I ripped it from its binding and fed it into the flames. Tears ran silently down my face. Staring blankly into the fire, I wished I could somehow erase the years of raw emotions, the constant teetering between hope and victories and anguish and sorrow, as easily as those pages were consumed by the fire.

Somewhere entangled in those struggles, somewhere between the lines, I agonized that there must be some hidden desire, some expectation that was against God's will. I wanted to take back the trust I had pledged to the Lord and scream in despair. That violent reaction epitomized my lifelong attitude; shoot first, aim later. A wiser woman would have mindfully reread those journals and drawn strength from the trust contained in those words.

With utter helplessness exposed and acknowledged, God faithfully steps in. He understands us. His nature being love, He is patient with us. He is not surprised by our weakness. God is able to do great things with us right where we are, even when we erroneously rage against or ignore Him. The heart speaks its own language, and we can be assured that it is heard. God is moved by our dependence on Him and by our faith. He keeps a record of our tears. He is aware of our pain. He took it with Him to the cross. The folly, the ugliness, and the sorrow fall away in His presence.

> "And He has said to me, 'My grace is sufficient for you, for power is perfected in weakness.' Most gladly, therefore, I will rather boast about my weaknesses, so that the power of Christ may dwell in me" (2 Cor. 12:9, NASB).

I was asked to write this by those whose lives were affected by my family's story, as well as by many who have heard it retold. I hope that I may connect with those who yearn for unconditional love, with those feeling pain and sorrow who are aching for relief and joy; so that they may know they are not alone. If you know my Lord and Savior Jesus Christ, you may recognize His voice in its telling. If not, my sincere prayer is that you would meet Him along the way. Just consider how my story might have looked had I not sought after Him for peace, hope, healing, and deeper understanding in my life.

Many voices tell this story. It is neither fact nor fiction. Although it is true for the one who is remembering. It is a collection of experiences telling a story of faith and the journey that I have come to find affected many others.

There is a universal hope held that we are not subject to senseless suffering. Greater minds than mine have pondered, reasoned, and debated this for centuries. Saint Gemma Galgani, a nineteenth century mystic, who developed the stigmata—or wounds of Christ—was quoted for having said, "If you really want to love Jesus, first learn to suffer, because suffering teaches you to love." For me, the joy in suffering was discovered in the presence of Jesus as I revisited my painful suppressed memories in His presence in my healing prayer.

I came to discover that much of my own misery was the work of the enemy, torturing me with lies and fear because of a vow or promise I had made to myself during a traumatic experience. Though made at a time when I did not know how to deal with the pain, it had unconscious power to bind me to a harsh reality. As I began to question why I thought the way I did and to pray about what I believed about the traumas in my life, I was led to amazing liberation.

Although those painful experiences may have been in my past, I learned that the inner vow made at that time of weakness, vulnerability, or immaturity had power to influence my thinking and behavior in the present. I was exhausted from my flesh wrestling with my desire to love as Jesus loved. I was able to be a nice person, but it didn't feel nice inside. Since discovering TPM and experiencing healing, I am now quick to turn to this prayer when I overreact knowing that my Savior waits for me and will show me the way to freedom. If I feel resistance to love or to forgive, I sense Jesus calling to me to turn to Him. Whereas it never would have occurred to me before, it now became my first impulse to pray for help.

Even now, I wonder if I have strength to write about what we had been through and have struggled so hard to put behind us. Countless people have said our story should be in a book, but I could not bring myself to do it. Yet the prompting would not go away. In the quiet of the night, I would often hear, "write it down," as soft as a whisper, but also as convicting as a decree.

It was not until years later, during my own health crisis that things changed. The receptionist from the Integrative Health Center (www.ihcenter.net) where I was being treated called me to say my doctor wanted me to make an appointment with Ed Lixey from Jehu Ministries International. He was a prophetic prayer intercessor who was scheduled by the health clinic to come and pray with their patients, and Dr. Coller wanted me to meet with him.

Although Ed Lixey didn't know me or our story, within moments of meeting, he declared he saw a book in me. There was power in the words he spoke to move me to action. Those same words I had resisted in the past, suddenly came alive in me, awakening the seed already planted in my heart. Slowly his words spread through my veins like fire until there was no doubt in my mind; I was writing a book. I had heard others say it many times before and my response had always been a sarcastic, "Sure, right," or "No, thanks," but not this time. When he proclaimed that I would write a book, the speaker's voice became my own and I agreed as if it had been my idea all along. It was the power of a spoken prophetic word.

Yes, I would write for God's own good purpose and to bring relief to this recurring, persistent persuasion. I realized I had become someone who would willingly crawl through broken glass to get this message into the hands of another young mom like me, who was praying for answers. A strong desire began to grow in my heart to encourage those struggling to find peace in a painful time in their life.

I became desperate to share what I had learned from my son's illness. I wanted some good to come from all we had been through. Then I received a call from a mother who was confused by an illness plaguing her beautiful, precious child. Soon after, another mom I spoke with expressed outrage at the severe treatment offered for her daughter for a chronic illness, all without a clear diagnosis.

It seemed as though overnight I began meeting moms whose young children were being diagnosed with adult diseases. From what they described, their children's body systems were not functioning as they should. I suspected that like my son, the sheer number of environmental toxins in our air, water, and food supply was overwhelming them. Many of the parents I spoke with wanted better options than the pharmaceuticals that were being offered by their medical doctors. They did not want to mask their child's symptoms by using medications with serious side effects. It was their gut feeling to refuse to believe that it was necessary to harm in order to heal.

I began praying for the families that came to me confused and uncertain of how to proceed. Although many loved their child's doctor, they had become disenchanted by the meager solutions they were offered. I was surprised how few knew about the benefits of detoxification and the transforming power of fresh, raw, organic whole food nutrition because it had become my entire world since changing the prognosis of my son's illness.

I was sympathetic to their frustration, as well as that of their doctor, fully understanding the limited time our current medical system allowed them to spend trying to untangle the menagerie of complicated symptoms. With confidence and from experience, I could recommend the benefits of finding a holistically trained health professional who not only understood how the body systems depend on each other and work together but also the preventative, nutritional, and integrative aspects of functional medicine. And I was certain God had a plan to use what we had learned to help others.

"Now to Him who is able to do far
more abundantly beyond all that we ask or

think, according to the power that works within us" (Eph. 3:20, NASB).

My purpose is to encourage those facing a crisis not to lose their faith but to ask God to lead them to the answers they need—to pray to know what He is asking them to do and to trust Him to show them what only He can do. We have the right and responsibility to direct our own health care. I pray that by sharing my journey I can bolster the confidence of others to consider the power of prayer and how optional, natural strategies can support the healing process to become well and remain well. I have learned there are many things that we can do, or stop doing, to vastly improve our family's health.

My goal is to help loosen the crippling fear of the unknown so that we may be free to move forward. I want it to be known that God has created and provided the remedy long before it was needed and that faith is an important part of healing and wholeness. Our healing journey will take us down many roads, and ultimately, we are all headed the same direction in the end. However, we can do much to enhance our quality of life by applying certain biblical principles to our journey. My message is to trust God for restoration and peace no matter what the present situation. Include Him on your journey. No matter where He leads you, He has the power to provide for you.

It became my dream to inspire a vision that would spread well beyond my family and my own sphere of influence. Our health is a gift from God that should not be neglected. I believe the enemy is attempting and, unfortunately, because we are not paying attention, succeeding in stealing it away as never before. However, God has a plan and it is a good one.

> "The thief comes only to steal and kill and destroy. I came that they may have life and have it abundantly" (John 10:10, ESV).

Standing left to right: Kathleen, David, Mary Beth,
Christine, Patti Ellen, Nicholas, and Brian.
Seated left to right: Donald, Germaine, Earl holding
Sharon, Ellen holding Thomas, Eileen (the author),
and Roger. Not pictured: Though always still with us,
Joey and baby Peter waiting for us in heaven.

CHAPTER 1
Faith

"He put another parable before them,
saying, 'The kingdom of heaven is like a
grain of mustard seed that a man took
and sowed in his field. It is the smallest
of all seeds, but when it has grown it
is larger than all the garden plants and
becomes a tree, so that the birds of the air
come and make nests in its branches.'"
—Matthew 13:31–32 (ESV)

Like our faith, the mustard seed though very small has the potential of amazing growth. I now know that I arrived here on earth with such a seed deep inside of me. It was born from the faithful and hard earned from the wayward, passed to me from generation to generation. My mustard seed of faith, initially nurtured then tested against the elements in the storms of rebellion, struggle, and pain until finally treasured in my heart, has ultimately borne its fruit in me.

It has taken me a long time, as healing often does, to realize that the fruit of my mustard seed of faith would be the strength I gained through my journey and now humbly share. This strength, like shelter for the birds that rest in the mature mustard tree's branches, is not for one but for many. It is my hope that the reader will also find rest here in these words, in the shade cast by our Creator—our Sustainer who causes the mustard seed's growth.

Sitting on a plane somewhere over the Atlantic, I reflect while on my way to see my eldest sister in Ireland. I can still remember the day she left in 1969 to study abroad. She remained in Ireland to marry the eldest of seven brothers and raise her five children there. For many years, I have ended our telephone conversations with, "Love you, see you soon!" and here I was finally experiencing what I envisioned every time we spoke. Was I programming my subconscious at the time, causing the universe to listen to my intention and attracting the means to accomplish it? I should not be surprised, for our faith demands it. Holy Scriptures tell us that we will receive what we speak and believe (Mark 11:22–24).

As children, we were served a daily dose of that concept at the breakfast table. Generally, it was oatmeal with a side of motivational speaker, Earl Nightingale. Sleepy-eyed at 6:00 a.m. in the morning, my large family were all summoned around our yellow laminate eight-foot-long kitchen table, made by dad's own hands out of a sheet of four-by-eight plywood and metal table legs. With a dozen children impressively assembled, each in their assigned seats, Dad would enthusiastically ask, "Okay! Who's happy?" The little one's hands would quickly shoot up, and the teenagers rolled their eyes. After saying the meals lengthy blessing, the cassette player clicked, and we heard Earl Nightingale, the author known as the "Dean of Personal Development," dish out advice with our nourishment.

My dad, a self-made businessman, attempted to school us from an early age on the power of positive thinking. And he did. We were all positive that we hated every minute of it! From the moment, the bedroom door cracked open in the morning and the light was switched on, we braced ourselves for it. "Wake up, sleepyheads. Rise and shine! It's time to whip your weight in wildcats!" Those who lagged behind were quickly deprived of their covers and a dousing of ice water awaited the hard learners.

If we only knew then, what we know now. Dad had already been up for hours. Not pausing to think of the long hours of work before him, his feet hit the floor with squats and push-ups to get his blood moving and body motivated. He spent the quiet predawn hours working in the office catching up on the piles of paperwork and the planning required for the myriad of businesses he owned. Landlord, builder, salesman, and farmer, his work was his prayer. It would provide for his large family as well as the three other extended families that in many ways, he helped to support. Beside his office door hung a framed image of a man's arm bent at the elbow with his sleeve rolled up and Dad's favorite motto beneath it reading, "I fight poverty. I work." Each of us learned in innumerable ways what that meant.

The boys became carpenters, mechanics, welders, and plumbers—friendly, dependable, and efficient—the kind that were the first to be called when a job needed to be done. From the youngest age, the girls earned money by nickels, dimes, and quarters for each batch of cookies, cakes, or pies they baked that were highly prized and praised by Dad and provided comfort after a long day's work. Dad in his wisdom would pull out his small notepad from his desk drawer or his shirt pocket. The inscription on its cover, along with his name and business address and phone number read "Nothing is impossible. Let me help you!" He would then enter the name of each pastry, the date and sum earned to keep until "payday" at the end of each month.

As we grew older and the kitchen no longer held our interest, the lure of a pay increase would send many of us to don overalls and grab a paintbrush or bucket to help the boys on the job. We were all well aware that if there was a job to be done and friends or cousins had come over to play, everyone, including guests, would be required to pitch in and help. The deal was sealed with the promise of a pop and a candy bar and of course the added benefit of the "sheer fun of it."

Dad insisted that breakfast, lunch, and dinner be eaten as a family and rarely was there an exception. Six in the morning, noon for the little ones at home, and again at 6:00 p.m. so he would regularly see his family. It was a respite from his eighteen-hour workdays, and I'm afraid that too often we did not do enough to bless him back for his dedication. Although he succeeded in teaching us how to work, I'm not sure we shared his enthusiasm for it. "Come on, this isn't work, this is fun!" he would exclaim as we followed alongside the hay wagon picking up bales of hay to heave onto the truck trailer or as we loaded the firewood, he cut from a felled tree. I think he had decided long ago that he would choose to see his heavy responsibilities and the work it took to meet them as a blessing and not a burden.

I was very young when I realized my father was a very important man to many people besides my family. It was Christmas time and he walked in the back door hollering, "Look what we have here!" He laid out a half-dozen plain white oversized shirt boxes on the kitchen counter. With great fanfare, he lifted the lids revealing piles of festively decorated Christmas cookies. We had never seen such confections! "Merry Christmas, from the tenants!" he beamed with pride, amid our squeals of delight.

It took a while though to understand the toll his responsibilities took on him physically. The lights on the touch-tone phone were the only thing illuminating the dark room where he finally sat down after coming in after sunset from a hard day's work. He began returning business calls that had come in while he was out. Climbing on his lap as a child, I would amuse myself winding the long spirals of the phone cord around my fingers while waiting for him to finish his conversation. A long silence followed by a loud beeping pulled my attention away from my play. I looked up to see he had nodded off mid-conversation, the beeping signifying that caller had long ago hung up. Taking the phone from his shoulder, I carefully placed the receiver back on the cradle trying not to disturb his soft snore.

It was not easy to put food on the table for such a large family and harder still to provide twelve years of private Catholic school education for each of us as well. My parents had an obvious deep respect for the Sisters of the

Immaculate Heart of Mary who were responsible for our education. Their dedication to providing a solid understanding of our faith was evident, and the discipline we learned would be something that would shape our lives. Whether I was carrying flowers in a procession for The Blessed Mother's May Crowning or being hurried out of our house when the IHM Sisters visited for a private swim in our indoor pool, I felt the sisters were part of our extended family.

Though not appreciated at the time, I now compare the enforced ritual of scheduled prayer in our home to a farmer preparing a plot of land for his garden. Our daily rosary, like the farmer regularly amending the soil to achieve the correct PH balance, helps to ensure a successful outcome. Like the diligent work of a farmer, prayer is an investment and a ready withdrawal of grace when needed.

Our family prayer time provided a systematic measuring, like fertilizing the soil year after year in preparation for the future harvest. Learning the best time to sow the seeds always increases the chance of the plants surviving. My parents knew that it was important to instill a discipline of prayer while we were young and that it would not fail to yield a harvest in our lives. The foundation my parents laid would become instrumental in helping me to find my way back to God when the road I strayed upon led me to a brick wall.

It was nothing short of a miracle that the planted Word of God kept the weeds of a rebellious adolescence from overcoming the work my parents invested in me. When I began taking responsibility for my faith and began reading the Bible, it helped clear my mind of years of wrong thinking. The more I relied on the wisdom I found in Scriptures to guide me as I raised my own family, the more sensitive I became to the way the Lord was leading me and it enlightened me to His remarkable timing.

I discovered the Word of God had the power to heal and change me. Learning to speak aloud His Word each time I needed to trust Him, I received His promised peace. Learning to surrender control strengthened my roots when the elements were against me. Faith calls those things that are not into being. I began to connect how the quiet time I spent with God in prayer prepared me for the future. Just as we might "put up" or can the produce from a garden for the winter months when fresh produce is less available, I found I had put up grace when my prayers came back to comfort me in my hardest trials.

> "Let us then with confidence draw near to the throne of grace, that we may receive mercy and find grace to help in time of need" (Heb. 4:16, ESV).

CHAPTER 2
Hope

"The Lord delights in those
who fear Him, who put their
hope in his unfailing love."
—Psalm 147:11 (NIV)

When tracing the roots of my family's faith, I did not need to look far to see the gift I have been given. I have glimpses of faith each time I reflect upon the lives of my parents and grandparents. The effects of their faith-filled lives have been left on their children's hearts. They are illustrated frequently through stories remembered and shared through the generations.

At first glance, our faith legacy may not be as easy to distinguish as our genetic inheritance, but it is there. We can readily see the resemblance of eyes, brow, and smile of our family members, but listening close to stories being told at a family reunion, I began to see other similarities as well. It appeared in a reoccurring phrase, inflection of voice, a declaration of hope, even in a disappointment or lingering sorrow. I discovered a trail of faith left by my ancestors that when prayerfully followed, provided a map of generational healing that had occurred in the past and even more that was waiting to take place. It revealed an opportunity for family blessings to take root where they may otherwise have been unknowingly missed or overlooked because of deep wounds or even neglect in continuing to sow those precious seeds of faith.

My maternal grandfather, Hiram Leon Joseph Patch, was born on April Fool's Day in 1898. Some say it was his birthright to have been bestowed with good humor, quick wit, and a fun-loving nature that would charm those around him wherever he went. Hiram grew up nearby to the fair-haired Elizabeth Veronica "Von" Waters and felt her tug on his heartstrings at a very young age. He was an independent young man at sixteen years old who was willing to lie about his age in order to enlist in the army and fight in the Great War. He was given the assignment of driving an ambulance through the treacherous French countryside. To distract himself from the agony of war, he would often dream of a future at home with his childhood sweetheart.

When the time came to return from his tour of duty, he was elated to think he would soon be renewing their friendship, confident that she felt the same. He wasted no time in making his way over to see her. Whistling a carefree tune, he wandered up the driveway to find Veronica sitting on her porch swing with another young fellow from down the street. Hiram grinned as he approached and shook the nervous suitor's hand. Awkwardly, the three sat sipping lemonade and making polite conversation all afternoon, both men reluctant to leave and give the other the advantage.

Finally, as dusk approached, the other boy observed it was getting late and timidly said good night before going home defeated. Hiram stayed through the evening and then promised to return the next day. Somewhere between his serenade of "Girl of My Dreams" and "My Wild Irish Rose," he had won her heart.

Von, as Elizabeth Veronica was called, had a deep faith and always knew she would raise her children Catholic. Her own mother, Ellen Mary Power, had instilled in her a great love for her Catholic faith. Von's grandparents had lived on a small farm in Ireland. During the English Occupation, her people were forbidden to speak the Irish language and were penalized if found practicing the Catholic faith.

Keeping their plans hidden from the authorities, her grandmother's cousin invited Catholics from farms nearby to come in the dark of night to her home where they would gather for Mass. Witnessing their act of faith and devotion to Jesus in the Holy Eucharist long before she fully understood its meaning caused Von's mother to profess she would not give up her faith for anyone or anything. Like her grandmother and mother, Von felt the same deep conviction in her own heart. Von was grateful that Hiram shared her Catholic faith. Their dependence on God in the hard times would in turn leave a lasting impression on their children.

Hiram was filled with ambition when he married Von, and to his great delight, he was soon offered a position playing the violin with the Toledo Philharmonic Orchestra. He often told her he felt like he was in another world when he was making music. Periodically, the opportunity arose to sit third violin for the Glen Gray and The Casa Loma Orchestra whenever they came to Toledo. However, it was a season of his life that unfortunately would not last. Though reluctant, he set aside his disappointment when it became all too evident that he would need to provide for his growing family as a bricklayer and not as a musician.

The sleepy town of Hopewell sat near the Ohio and Michigan border and seemed like a wonderful place to Hiram and Von to raise my mother Ellen and her siblings. For two years, they lived in a small garage while Hiram built their new home. Brick by brick, he laid his hopes and dreams into that house. He envisioned the permanence of his solid little house as he chiseled his family name of "Patch" into the foundation.

The year was 1929. As news of the stock market crash spread, banks closed. Without warning, his life's savings was gone, and the bank called his loan. He realized he was on the verge of losing their home. Lining up with the other men in town, he showed up for odd jobs whenever they were available. Subsisting on canned jam and wild game, they struggled as so many others did to survive during the Great Depression.

Unaware of the turn of world events as a young adolescent, my mother Ellen wandered along their property's edge waiting for her sisters to finish their chores and join her outside. She heard her father's voice ahead in the tall grass as he mumbled a familiar stream of cuss words beneath his breath. "Daddy?" she called. Hiram lifted his head and grinned. "Ah, Ellen. Good! Come on over here." Following her father's voice, she found him squatting in the ditch and peering into the culvert. "Yes, Daddy?" Taking her hand, he led her to a fallen log a few feet away. Picking up his rifle, he placed it in her hands, showing her quickly how to hold and fire it as he explained, "I'm going to chase that rabbit out of the drain, and when you see it, I want you to shoot it!" Though her eyes widened in disbelief at his idea, she nodded and clamped her mouth in a hard line to keep from questioning him.

Aiming at the hole, she steadied herself, hesitating only a moment when the rabbit bolted from his hiding place. When it paused at the sight of her, she pulled the trigger. She shuddered as the explosion sent the rabbit flying. Although she had helped secure their dinner for the evening meal, she prayed she would never have to do that again.

Soon it became all too evident the meager work in the area would not allow them to remain where they were. "Mother," he tenderly called his young bride, "we can't go on like this." Hiram sighed, looking far into the distance. He and Von held hands and watched as the evening sun and their dreams faded away. Nodding sadly, Von squeezed his hand. They would give up their home and move on.

Opportunity led Hiram north to Temperance, Michigan. By its name, you may not have guessed it would be the choice of this brick-laying, whiskey-drinking true Irishman at heart to settle with his bride and five young children. With what was left of his war bonus, he managed to purchase a property to split between himself and his good friend Clint Smalley. As bricklayer and carpenter, they were determined to find a way to build a future and a home for their families. They discovered through a friend working for the Michigan Central Railroad that plans were being made to demolish some old, unused buildings. In a bold business barter, Hiram and Clint offered to take down the buildings in exchange for the lumber, which they would then use to build both of their homes.

Taking in stride all they had been through, the Patches soon filled their small new home with music and laughter again. Working together, they made their little place a haven in the hard times. It became a home where honesty and the ability to spin a yarn were equally valued. Von and her children faithfully attended Mass every Sunday at Saint Anthony Parish in the nearby town. When the weather was harsh, they followed the railroad tracks holding hands so they would not lose their way.

They were devout in their faith, and it saddened the girls at times when Hiram would not attend Mass with his family. When asked why their daddy was not going with them to church, Von explained in hushed tones that he had only one pair of trousers that were beyond repair. He promised he would join them as soon as he got a job and something decent to wear. Still it did not occur to the girls that they were poor. They were grateful for the blessings they faithfully counted each day.

After a time, Hiram did fulfill his promise. The girls came down the stairs early one Sunday morning to find him standing at the front door wearing the suit he purchased at the local general store. When the girls whispered that it looked like it might be too big for him, he grinned and winked, declaring, "That's great! Then there's room for me to grow into it!"

The three sisters felt like angels singing in the choir in front of their dad. Ellen sang a rich alto harmony to Alicia's and Germaine's sweet soprano. The girls beamed at their father's praise following Mass. Proud of their gifted singing, it would not be long before their dad would be persuaded to play his violin at church alongside them for very special occasions.

The children were taught by example and very few words. Von was generous, kind, and happy through the worst of conditions. She never showed disappointment and she seemed to naturally accept life just as it was. Her strength and faith made her daughters want to grow up to be just like her. The gentleness and kindness Von passed onto her daughters were learned from her own mother. Von had witnessed the generosity her mother had shown to a neighbor who had been shunned by others in their community. When the county's wells began to dry up and yet theirs still ran with water, she believed it was because of her mother's act of love toward her neighbor and her trust in God that caused their small farm to be spared.

My mother, Ellen Mary Patch, was just five years old when she felt the first seeds of faith growing in her heart. She skipped happily into the kitchen at her mother's call that day. "Ellen Mary, I need you to run across to the neighbors and fetch your brothers home for dinner for me, please." Not wanting to go out alone, Ellen was filled with trepidation. Looking up at her mother, she hesitated, "But . . ." She had never ventured out alone across the field before! She did not want to do it. Von, wiping her hands on her apron, bent her slight frame over her eldest daughter.

Sensing her uneasiness, she took Ellen's face gently in her hands. "It's all right. Jesus will go with you."

Ellen decided then, never doubting the truth of what her mother spoke, that Jesus was indeed with her. She straightened her spine and turned to set off directly. Her hand squeezed tightly at her side, she declared as much to herself as anyone else, "Come on, then, Jesus!" Smiling and humming, she skipped contentedly out the door to help her mother by calling in her brothers.

Hiram was a fine bricklayer and stonemason, a good husband, father, and neighbor, and trustworthy friend. He taught his children to be honest and honorable as well as providing a daily example of when and how to cuss. With his quick wit and infectious humor, Hiram often appeared as if by cue onto the stage of their daily life to keep their spirits up.

One Sunday morning, as they walked home from Mass, the family wandered past their small garden beside the house. Noticing that the sun had dried the dew on the ripening strawberries, Hiram suggested they fill a bucket of the fresh fruit to bring inside for their lunch. With Von's reluctant agreement and a stern warning to mind they keep their clothes clean, the girls ran to the shed bringing out containers for everyone.

Carefully choosing the ripest ones to be mashed into jam, the girls excitedly filled their baskets. But soon it was apparent their brothers had lost interest in the chore and found another use for the berries. Scolding them as she ducked from an airborne fruit, Von warned them to stop immediately so they would not soil their Sunday clothes.

Foolishly ignoring her instruction, the rambunctious boys quickly found themselves lifted from their crouched position in the garden row and deposited with a splash into the nearby water trough. "Hey!" the boys hollered and sputtered at their dad. Covering their mouths, the girls giggled with glee at the boys' fate. Without a word, Hiram winked at his bride and cheerfully whistling, continued down the row.

During harsh weather in the north, brickwork was steady only during the mild months unless a fireplace or wall job could be found somewhere indoors. Although it was difficult to make ends meet, it left valued time for Hiram to be at home with his family. Gathering around the fire at night, they would make music together, the strains of the fiddle and happy harmonies seeping through the cracks in the windowpane echoing across the moonlit snow.

Von depended on her faith and prayer to sustain and comfort her, especially when it was necessary for Hiram to travel to find work. One such stormy night after the children were tucked into bed, she sat near the potbelly wood stove to begin her night vigil of prayer. The storm had intensified, and she flinched when she saw lightning strike in the field outside the window.

Fervently praying for the safety of all her loved ones, she suddenly felt herself picked up from beneath her arms and deposited into the chair across the room. A crash of thunder shook the house, and smoke and sparks flew from the stones beneath the nearby stove where moments ago she had been sitting. The room illuminated an eerie green glow. Crossing herself, she thanked the Lord. It was not the first time that she witnessed angelic intervention, and it would not be the last.

> "For He will give His angels charge concerning you, to guard you in all your ways. They will bear you up in their hands, that you do not strike your foot against a stone" (Ps. 91:11–12, NASB).

Ellen admired her mother's gentleness and yearned to be like her. Knowing she was a witness to her mother's instruction and example, she strove very early to imitate her in response to everyday occurrences. Ellen was still very young when she learned that following her first impulse could lead her to say and do things she would later regret. She prayed to be filled with wisdom and she soon learned that life would give endless opportunities for her to show mercy and love.

One winter morning, as they walked briskly through town on a holiday errand, Ellen held her mother's hand, bristling with excitement. The Christmas decorations gaily displayed in the store windows drew a gasp of pleasure from Ellen, her footsteps slowing until she paused directly in front of the general store. There, perched jauntily in the window, was an authentic Shirley Temple doll. The doll was dressed exactly as Ellen had seen the child star in the Hollywood blockbuster *Bright Eyes*. The crisp red polka dot dress sparkled, the ringlets of blond hair curled tightly to the doll's head. Ellen ached to know what it would feel like to hold the doll in her arms. She found herself wondering if she would ever have one of her very own. Knowing it was completely impossible for her family to splurge on such an extravagant purchase, she sighed and let her mother lead her on their way.

Early the next morning, the family gathered around the tree to exchange humble Christmas gifts. Ellen's eyes widened as her mother handed her a large long box wrapped in plain brown paper. Meeting her mother's eyes with hope, she slowly tore off a small corner of the paper, exposing the box and revealing the small shoes of a doll. She held her breath as she slid her fingers inside the paper, slowly freeing—not the Shirley Temple doll she had her heart set on—but nonetheless a porcelain doll all the same. Carefully schooling her disappointment before she lifted her eyes, Ellen smiled up at her mother and thanked her profusely for such a thoughtful and expensive gift.

Later that day when friends came over to visit, the children decided to go down to the frozen pond to skate on the ice. Upon seeing Ellen's new doll, the youngest of their friends asked if she could stay inside with Ellen's little sister, Germaine, to play with the doll. Reluctantly Ellen granted permission. Within minutes, the two littlest girls joined the others on the ice. "What did you do with my doll?" Ellen asked with apprehension. Casually shrugging her shoulders, the ill-mannered child skated off.

Dread filled Ellen's heart as she slid to the snowbank, quickly removed the blades from her boots, and ran home. Stepping inside the front door, her worse fears were realized. Her new doll lay on the floor broken apart in sections, the rubber bands that previously held it together dangling from the arms and legs. Doubling over in anger, a wail came from somewhere deep within her as she screamed, "I'll kill her! I'll kill her!" From across the room, Ellen's grandfather poked his head up from the newspaper he was reading. "Here now, what's this all about?"

"She broke my doll! I'll kill her! I'll kill her!" Ellen screamed. The sound of her own words felt like a cold slap to her heart, stunning her with the intensity. Walking quickly to her side and taking her by the hand, her grandfather led her over to the broken doll. "There, there. I understand you are upset, but you don't really want to kill your friend, do you?"

Ellen knelt on the floor and sadly looked at the broken pieces in front of her. Remembering her mother's happiness at being able to surprise her with a doll (even though sadly it was not the one she really wanted) caused her to pause. "No, I guess not." She shrugged. She instinctively knew her anger could not repair the damage and would only spoil the day and her mother's thoughtfulness.

"Here, I'll fix it!" her grandfather said optimistically. She sat next to him at the kitchen table as he took a roll of yellowing masking tape from the kitchen drawer and taped the doll's arms and legs to the body until it looked like a mummy. Tugging the dress back over its head, he handed her the doll grinning with mischievous delight. "There now, she's good as new!" Staring dubiously at the ridiculous looking doll, she decided right then and there that nothing would ever be worth getting that upset over again. From a very young age, Ellen had learned the importance of kindness and forgiveness, and now she knew she wanted peace more than any object she desired.

As they grew to adulthood, the bond between Ellen and her sisters flourished. They were best friends and constant companions and deeply cherished one another. Like her mother, Ellen attracted the attention of the young men going off to war. Like many others, she was quick to give hope to the young men that they would return. She soon accepted the friendship ring of a young sailor. However, the relationship didn't last long. Ellen discovered the young man whispering to a giggling schoolgirl at the church social one night. A sudden distrust growing inside her, she marched over, returned the ring without a word and turning on her heel rejoined her sisters.

In the somber climate of the war effort, there was little cause for gaiety even among the young people. Ellen felt the pang of separation when her two older brothers, Vick and Hal, left their work in the fields to join in the fight, one to the navy, the other the marines. Therefore, when the church announced it would give its sons a proper sendoff, the girls were excited to join in the festivities. The three sisters sat chatting on a bench in the church hall when a hush fell over the room. A dashing U.S. Marine in full attire entered and stood casually viewing the crowd. When his eyes fell upon Ellen, he strode directly over to her to introduce himself. Confidently he asked to see her as much as he could before he shipped out. By the third date, he had given her a ring.

Trusting that God had a plan for her life and would reveal it in time, she asked to keep their engagement secret until he returned. He was to be stationed in Hawaii for training before being shipped out for duty. Since they frequently exchanged letters, she became uneasy when her letters began to be returned unopened. Six months later, her fears were confirmed. She overheard the neighbors talking about the tragedy.

Many knew of Ellen and the young marine's friendship, but none knew of their secret engagement; therefore, it did not occur to his family in their grief to notify her when his ship was bombed on the way to the Philippines. He never came home. She gravely accepted the news. She turned her own sadness over to God and prayed for the comfort of his family. She had given her life to be directed by God and trusted He would find the right man for her at the right time.

DIVINE APPOINTMENT

The heat was breaking records that steamy July afternoon in 1944 when my dad, Earl Wickenheiser, first saw my mom. Ellen had arrived with her family for the celebration and dedication of the World War II Memorial Board in downtown Monroe. She had not wanted to go that day, but her father convinced Ellen to come with them and sing in the church choir. Doing her best to put on a good face, she had donned her lightest cotton print dress, her chestnut brown hair tied back from the hot sun.

Earl had already arrived to represent the National Guard in the dedication ceremony. He was left behind when his brothers went off to war. Trying all five services, he too had attempted to enlist, but he was unable to pass the eye exam. Though disappointed, he was glad to be welcomed into the National Guard.

He had ridden his motorcycle into town that day because he was scheduled to lead the Guards in a motor brigade. Waiting for the other Guards to arrive and trying to escape the heat, he sat on the running board of a car in the church parking lot in the shade of a large maple tree. The quaint city of Monroe was bustling with locals and visitors alike as they lined the bridge that crossed the murky Raisin River that ran through the center of town. The heat was no obstacle for those who were hoping for the best advantage to watch the parade, the town's tribute to the fallen soldiers.

Earl stood and leaned casually against the side panel of the car surveying the gathering crowd hoping to recognize one of his troops among them. His eyes fell upon the figure of a slender young woman, and though he only glimpsed her silhouette, he thought she must be the prettiest gal there. He knew instantly that he wanted to meet her. Waiting for her to turn, he found himself saying, "I'm going to marry that girl." The thought seemed to drop into his mind as though an angel from above had cast a fishing line into his thoughts and the bait was taken.

Not knowing how he could arrange to meet her, he was suddenly inspired to pray she would faint so he could go to her rescue. Like a well-orchestrated play, he stared in awe as if a curtain had parted and the object of his admiration unbelievably swayed and slumped slowly to the ground.

He was propelled across the street and shouldering his way through the gathering crowd quickly offered, "Can I help?" At her father's nod, he assisted in carrying Ellen to the temporary first aid room that had been set up nearby.

Moments after she was revived, Ellen asked for an aspirin and a glass of water to soothe her pounding head. Earl overheard her mother relaying to her father that there was nothing available and he promptly spoke up, "I can fix that!" He offered to go quickly on his motorcycle to get aspirin for her at the drugstore down the street. When Earl returned, he resumed his post in the hall waiting patiently until he could talk to her. Stubbornly and doing her best to avoid him, Ellen stayed in the room hoping Earl would leave. Well, after the parade dedication had ended, her mother, Von, came in to say it was time for them to leave.

"You have to get up, Ellen. Everyone else is gone and this nurse wants to go home now." She strongly encouraged Ellen to show good manners and thank the young man who had gotten her the aspirin. "Yes, I suppose I do need to thank him," she said, reluctantly obeying her mother, as she rose and followed her out the door. Finding Earl cheerfully exchanging banter with her father in the hall, Ellen offered her hand and murmured her thanks. Smiling in reply, Earl turned to her father. "Well, you know, Mr. Patch, Carleton is just ten miles away and they are having a homecoming tonight. Why don't you bring your family out there, have some refreshment and a bite to eat? You could meet my mother and some of the family." Hiram considered the impressive young man's suggestion. Then to Ellen's utter dismay, her father answered, "Yeah . . . I guess that would be all right." Bristling inside at her predicament, Ellen could only stare in disbelief. "What in the world is my father thinking!" she wondered.

Coincidentally, they pulled into the parking lot just as Earl's family arrived at the homecoming. After making the introductions and a few minutes of conversation, Earl said, "I would like to run home and change out of this Guard uniform quick. Is it all right if Ellen rides with me?" He motioned toward the motorcycles where his friend Don was standing talking with his girlfriend Florine. "My friends will come with us!" Her father considered a moment before replying, "Yeah, I guess that would be all right."

Ellen looked skeptically at her father. She had never gone against him before. Although she wanted to refuse, she did not have the courage to cry out, "No! I'm not going!" and instead she reluctantly agreed. Settling behind Earl on his motorcycle, her mind raced at the preposterous idea of being sent with a veritable stranger to his house. Obviously, Earl's mother and family would not be there. Bristling, she wondered, "Had everyone lost their minds?"

They turned from the road into the driveway of a large white clapboard-sided house that sat at the top of a slight hill. They filed in the back door and into the tidy kitchen. Florine paused beside the kitchen table where a clean white dishtowel lay draped across a large pan. "Hey, Earl! What's this?" Florine asked. Lifting the edge, he replied, "It's my birthday cake." "Oh, today is your birthday!" she exclaimed. "Happy Birthday, Earl!"

Ellen rolled her eyes and thought, "Of course, it was his birthday. How convenient. He'd better not think he's getting anything from me!"

"Hey, Ellen, your dad said you play the piano. Why don't you sit there and play, and Florine can sing. I'll go upstairs with Don and we'll change out of our uniforms. We'll be right back."

Stepping into the front parlor, Ellen sat alongside Florine on the bench. Opening the piano book, they began leafing through the pages. Choosing "Red Sails in the Sunset," they began to sing. When they realized they had sung every song in the book, they wondered why the young men had delayed coming back downstairs. Little did they realize that Earl and Don had purposefully waited just so the girls would keep on playing and they could enjoy their performance.

Later that week, an unfamiliar car pulled up in Ellen's driveway.

Her mother called out, "Ellen, that young man is here to see you!"

Looking up from the book she was reading and peering out the window, she said, "How do you know he's here to see me?"

"Of course, he's here to see you!" her mother exclaimed. "Don't you want to change?"

Looking down at her shorts and halter, bare feet tucked beneath her, she flippantly remarked, "No, if he doesn't like me as I am, he can just leave or get used to it!" Unconcerned at her mother's chagrin, she rose and went to the door. Stepping out onto the porch, Ellen waited. Earl crossed the lawn and removing the fedora from his head, he greeted her.

Looking intently at Ellen, he grinned.

"What?" she inquired, her face reddening.

"I'm going to marry you," he stated.

"What do you mean? You don't even know me!" she scoffed in astonishment.

"Oh, I know you all right," he replied. "And I'm going to marry you."

Folding her arms across her chest, "We'll see about that!" she retorted with a bit more force than she meant, the disappointments from her past casting an understandable shadow on her enthusiasm.

Earl did know her. He listened to her father praise his daughter and her accomplishments for three hours that day out in the hall while waiting for her to leave her hiding place in the infirmary. At nearly twenty years old, Ellen knew it was time to leave her father's house and begin her own family. She trusted her father's judgment, she trusted God, and she was learning to trust Earl. What more did she need?

Several months passed and Earl continued the courtship of Ellen. Her father approved of him, so she was willing to get to know him. Both began to believe that their meeting was divinely inspired. Ellen admired Earl's persistence and gradually was learning to love him. She was impressed by how he treated his family. Before long, Earl properly proposed to Ellen and then asked her father's permission to marry. With her parents' approval, she surrendered her heart to him.

The wedding date was set for January 13, 1945. They would marry at Saint Anthony's Parish in Temperance, Michigan. On the morning of the wedding, Ellen stood solemnly in the church corridor with her sisters and mother. The guests were seated and waiting in the pews. The time for the service to begin arrived, but Earl and his family had not. At thirty minutes past the appointed hour, the next scheduled wedding party began to arrive, and her own guests began getting restless. Ellen's mother finally asked, "Ellen, what are you going to do?"

Ellen considered the other bride and her family waiting, even now some of them assembled out in the cold on the church steps, and said, "I'm going to wait five more minutes and then I'll just go home." Four minutes passed on the clock on the wall when the doors of the church flew open and Earl burst into the foyer with his large family filing in behind him.

Another whole drama had been playing out at the Wickenheiser home. Rushing to get out the door of the house, Earl's young sister Theresa, in her bridesmaid finery, brushed carelessly past her siblings. As she scrambled down the frost-covered porch stairway, her foot slid off the last icy step. Flying through the air, Theresa landed flat on her stomach in the mud. More embarrassed than hurt, she cried out in disappointment that her dress was ruined.

"Nonsense!" Her eldest sister Clara announced, "I'll wash it and iron it dry. It won't take long." Certain that all would be well, she assured Theresa, "They will wait."

After the hasty explanations, the marriage service began. Though the priest hurried through the ceremony for the sake of the waiting bridal party, it would be a memorable day for Ellen. It would be memorable not for romantic, sentimental, or fanciful reasons but because she took her vows seriously. Standing before God, she promised for life until at death do they part, she would honor and love the man she felt God had chosen for her. Earl had found his prize. A woman of faith, who without letting emotion cloud her judgment, understood patience and trusted everything would always work out in the end.

Ellen respected the man that she married. She knew in her heart that Earl would be a good provider for their future family. Earl was just twenty-five years old, but for the last few years, a heavy responsibility had fallen on him. While his brothers went off to fight in the war, Earl was already providing for his widowed mother and five sisters.

Soon after the war began, the unthinkable happened. Tragedy struck his aunt and uncle, leaving their cousins orphaned. Earl's commitment increased when his mother took in five of the young children into their home. Ellen knew that Earl loved having a large family and that he would be a good father. She promised herself that when the time came, she would impart to her own children how Earl's sincere dedication to his family enabled him to carry such a heavy responsibility.

As the war continued, Earl found work making machine parts at Alco Aluminum Factory. Leaving from work, he would go directly to check in first with his mother and siblings before going home to have supper with his bride. One evening, dinner prepared and getting cold, Ellen became concerned as the usual time for Earl to arrive home came and went. Sitting alone, she stared at the phone wondering why he didn't call and what could possibly have happened. She continued to watch the kitchen clock until deciding that worry would not bring him home any sooner. Turning off the stove, she began to put away his dinner. After cleaning up the dishes in the sink, she sat down to wait. It was near midnight when she finally saw the car headlights reflected in the front window.

Meeting Earl as he entered the back door, Ellen asked, "Where have you been?"

Sheepishly, he replied, "Out to mom's."

"Why for so long?"

With hat in hand, he explained that he saw to it that the kids were washed up, homework completed and in bed, and then became completely engrossed in the chores and repairs that needed attention.

Noticing how late it had become, his mother had asked, "Earl, aren't you going to go home?"

"Home?" he inquired. "Oh, yeah. Home!" Though just newlywed, he had unbelievably forgotten that he was married. Ellen shook her head and laughed sending up a prayer of thanksgiving for his safety. "I'm relieved to hear everything was all right!" she said. She realized then that it was God's grace that had matched them so well. It made her chuckle to think how another woman might have reacted to such an admission.

It was not long before his entrepreneurial spirit led Earl to venture into sales. Excited at the prospect, he secured an interview for a position at Weather Seal Storm Windows and Doors in Toledo, Ohio. Ellen was pleased when he invited her to come along with the promise of a lunch out on the town.

They left promptly at 9:00 a.m. to be sure to make his eleven o'clock appointment. Finding a parking space around the block from the Weather Seal office, he instructed Ellen to wait in the car and he would be back shortly to take her to eat when he was through with his appointment.

An hour passed. Without anyone in sight and nothing else to do, as was her habit to fill the time, Ellen began to pray her rosary. Before long, she had prayed another, then another and another. Five hours had somehow passed when Earl finally came hurrying around the corner of the building and quickly approached the car.

Puzzled, she asked, "Where have you been?" as he opened her door.

"I'm sorry! I forgot I had you with me!" he said winking and making her laugh.

Stirred with excitement to tell his story, he explained that when the interview was done, they invited him to meet the boss for lunch to become better acquainted. He talked to them about his interest in windows and doors all afternoon. When it was all said and done, the job was his! She congratulated Earl, proud of him for diligence, tenacity, and fortitude. She was pleased and certain that her time of prayerful solitude played a part in his success.

To some it might seem that leaving her to her own devices for so long was a sign of an inconsiderate man, insensitive to his wife's feelings and needs. To Ellen, it was the sign of a hard worker and good provider, a determined man who would not give up until he got the job that would benefit his family. She did not consider her feelings to be more important than the family's welfare.

> "A wife of noble character who can find? She is worth far more than rubies. Her husband has full confidence in her and lacks nothing of value"
> Prov. 39:10–11 (NIV)

CHAPTER 3
Love

"For God so loved the world, that
He gave His only Son, that whoever believes in Him should not
perish but have eternal life."
—John 3:16 (ESV)

It was a different world in 1945 when my parents, Earl and Ellen, married. Dad had his heart set on a dozen children, although Mom thought three would be more to her liking. It was a serendipitous compromise that resulted in their family of fifteen. I was named Eileen Therese, the twelfth of fifteen children born to Earl and Ellen Mary (Patch) Wickenheiser in Monroe, Michigan. Their meeting was a story of love and commitment that has been told and retold. Dad was the third oldest of nine brothers and sisters. Mom was the middle of five. For Dad, it was love at first sight. Mom on the other hand admitted having her doubts. It is the grace of God that brought them together, and faith and faithfulness that kept them together.

The peace Mom carried in her heart was evident in everything she did. She took solitude in her prayer time, as each opportunity presented itself. If she turned her back from the children for more than a moment or had to run downstairs for something, she would quickly say a prayer for the Lord to watch over them. Each day while the kids slept or when traveling in the car, she would pray the rosary. When leaving her children in the care of others, she had a simple philosophy that kept her from worrying: "I have said my prayers. As long as they are not getting hurt or hurting each other, then everything is all right."

Ellen was very young when she first felt the call to motherhood. She found deep satisfaction and fulfillment in her vocation. She was aware that along with the blessings of having many children, there would also be challenges and heartbreak, still she welcomed the responsibility. With grace, she accepted it all, living in the present moment while still cherishing her precious memories.

We all have memories that seem to be imprinted on our hearts. We can easily relive those events, feeling much like we did at the time they happened. Faces, colors, scents, and sounds are painted in minute detail. In the trying times especially, it is important to be conscious of what takes root in our heart. There is a very distinct connection between our past experiences, the beliefs we form and how power-fully those beliefs influence our life.

An Emory University School of Medicine study has shown how a traumatic event could affect the DNA in sperm and alter the brains and behavior of subsequent generations. It could be overwhelming to think that we may carry that imprint until we realize the power of our faith. According to Christian neuroscientist Dr. Caroline Leaf, neuroplasticity is a new scientific discovery proving that we can literally change our brains through our thoughts and choices. We can physically create new neural pathways and destroy old ones. We can wire out toxic beliefs and thinking patterns and wire in truths. When looking at my childhood family portrait, I see in my mind the missing faces of both of my brothers who had been born and tragically died before I knew them, and they feel as real to me as my siblings captured in black and white in that photograph. What I believe now about our family's tragic loss has been changed in the light of God's Word.

> "The spirit of the Lord God is upon me, because the Lord has anointed me; He has sent me to bring good news to the afflicted to bind up the brokenhearted, to proclaim liberty to the captives, release to the prisoners, to announce a year of favor from the Lord and a day of vindication by our God; to comfort all who mourn" (Isa. 61:1–2, NABRE).

A milestone year for our family was 1956. The property that backed up against the tree-lined Stoney Creek would be perfect for Dad and his sister's family to split and build homes for their growing families. It could not have made my mom happier to know her kids would grow up with their cousins right next door. She counted her blessings daily and dedicated each one of us to the Sacred Heart of Jesus and the Immaculate Heart of Mary. Mom understood her dependence on the grace of God. This knowledge gave her peace when things were beyond her control. No matter what was happening in her life or around her, Mom always imagined herself plugged into that grace. She believed that choosing each day to remain in that place of grace prepared her for whatever might lie ahead.

One autumn afternoon, returning from the funeral of a dear friend's young daughter, another of Mom's premonitions began. As she contemplated how hard it must be for anyone to lose a child, she began to pray her rosary. As she prayed with eyes closed, she visualized a photo album on her lap, each page displaying the face of one of her children. She began to pray for each child by name as the page turned to the next in line. First Nick, then Dave, Pat, Chris, Mary Beth, and Kathleen until quite unexpectedly, she sensed the book slam shut. "That's strange," she thought. "Five-year-old Joey's picture should be next." The vision was beyond her understanding. Keeping the experience to herself, she continued to pray for Joey, Brian, and Roger, trusting God to reveal the meaning if necessary.

A few months later on a Saturday evening, Earl announced there would be a family outing to visit Ellen's sister Alicia the next morning after church. It was a rare and wonderful occasion to visit the Oldham cousins. It was a joy for Ellen to see her sister who, having nine children of her own, gave my mother unfailing support and encouragement. That night, Ellen was fairly singing in anticipation as she gave her three littlest boys a bath. Hearing summer thunder in the distance, she bent over the tub to finish washing up the baby who was centered between Brian on one side and Joey near the faucet.

Quite unexpected, Joey stood up leaning on the water spout for support. Catching his movement, she lifted her head to see her son's face drain of color, his body quiver and forcefully slump against the wall. Gasping and calling on the Mother of God for help, she felt something like electrical shock go through her as Joey slumped over her outstretched arm. Their mother's startling cry brought the older girls running. "Get the little boys," she instructed with unearthly calm. Undeterred by the terrified faces around her, she lifted Joey from the water wrapping a towel around his limp body. With each step down the hallway, her voice intensified in clarity, volume and urgency "Earl . . . Earl! Earl!" Meeting him midway through the kitchen, Ellen breathlessly related as best she could what she thought had happened.

Holding Joey close to her chest, she dropped into the kitchen chair rocking him gently back and forth, praying in earnest. Her mind began racing as she heard Dad instructing his oldest son to run next door and tell his sister Rosemary to come quickly. Dialing the phone, he called the closest help available, Mr. Townsend, a rescue fireman and close friend, who said he would meet them at the hospital. Ellen's heart pounded uncontrollably belying her apparent calm as her mind wailed, "Why doesn't Earl hurry! He's dying, he's dying!"

Earl's final orders were thrown over his shoulder for the children to clean up the water and get ready for bed. He told his oldest daughter they were taking Joey to the hospital and finally lifted Mom from the chair and lead her to the car. Neither dared to say a word and the silence hung heavy, the trees blurring as they passed. In minutes, they arrived at the emergency room entrance.

In the space of a moment, Ellen found herself standing next to the gurney, looking down in misery and shock, listening as her son was pronounced dead upon arrival. She vaguely heard Mr. Townsend shout, "Wait!" as he rushed to their side, valiantly attempting to resuscitate Joey while Earl's desperate pleas implored him not to stop, pleading that he not give up. Endless minutes passed until sadly shaking his head, Mr. Townsend slowly backed away. An anguished cry caught in Earl's throat as he bowed his head close to Joey's colorless face, his heart wrenching as he bitterly wept over his son.

In shock and trembling in her grief, Ellen reached out touching her husband gently on his arm. It was the first and would be the last that she would ever see him cry. A vision then filled her mind. She saw Joey evolving from a small toddler into a young man dressed in priestly vestments. It was the same image that had startled Earl from his sleep just a few weeks earlier, causing him to share what he had seen with her. Now, she saw it clearly herself.

> "Before I formed you in the womb I
> knew you, before you were born, I set you
> apart; I appointed you as a prophet to the
> nations" (Jer. 1:5, NIV).

Ellen next found herself in her kitchen trying to remember exactly how she had gotten home. She heard Earl order the children out of the room and dial the telephone to notify her mother. "Von, there has been an accident and we have terrible news." He relayed what had happened and that they had no clear reason as to why. There wasn't any way to tell if the shock that caused Joey's heart to stop was an undetected heart condition or an electrical malfunction in the grounding of the new house. His own voice finally chocking, he said, "I'm putting Ellen on the phone. She needs you now." The sound of her mother's voice calling out to her as she raised the receiver to her ear caused Ellen's composure to crumble. She folded into Dad's arms weeping in grief and cried, "Mama, he's gone. Our little Joey is gone!"

Standing to the side, nine-year-old Christine clung to the doorframe watching the heartbreaking scene unfold. Catching a movement out of the corner of her eye, she spied little Brian clinging tightly to the metal leg beneath the kitchen table, terrified of his mother's sobs. Christine crouched down to his level, quietly coaxing him to come to her. Although he shook his head repeatedly, he finally stood and toddled out, wrapping his arms securely around her neck and burying his face in the blanket of soft red curls on her shoulder. Soothing him in a hushed voice, she slowly backed out of the room to join the others huddled on the living room sofa.

The arrangements were made without delay. Instead of engaging the funeral home for visitation, Dad insisted that Joey be laid out at home. The squeak in the front door announced a steady stream of family and friends stopping by to share the family's grief. Stoically, Ellen responded automatically to each visitor with words of faith and acceptance even as her heart was aching. She provided a steady reply to those who sought to comfort her, "I accept every-thing as the will of God. This is no exception. Mother told me early in my marriage, 'When you give birth to your children, remember that they first belong to God.' For unknown reasons, He has taken Joey back to Himself, who am I to disagree?"

Hearing repeatedly that he was such a special boy, Mom thought how well she knew it to be true. She could still feel the heaviness of her arms from the hours she held Joey through the night, as her infant suffered colic. Ellen would carry him to the far corner of the living room, hop-ing not to disturb the sleeping household. Pacing the floor one night, she realized that Joey would become still as they passed the spot where the family prayed their rosary each morning in front of the shrine of the Blessed Mother of Jesus. His cries would cease and gazing up at the statue of Our Lady of Fatima, his little body would relax, and he would finally fall asleep. Every precious hour that she had held Joey was now imprinted forever on her heart.

Ellen recalled how much fun it was to watch him play. He was such a unique little guy. If a toy were taken away from him, he would just smile and let it go. Though he spoke very little, he would sing as he banged on pots and pans, playing happily on the kitchen floor. Upon seeing his father driving his truck and trailer out of the driveway, he would pretend to do the same. He would drape his sister's toy iron over his shoulder, dragging it on the floor behind him. If asked, "Joey, what are you doing?" he would just turn and happily smile.

For the longest time in stolen moments, when her emotions threatened to overwhelm her, Ellen would quietly slip into the bathroom and muffle her anguished sobs in a towel. In her attempt to protect her children from the intensity of her grief, she cried out her pain in that private sanctuary. After two years of braving her daily life and secretly grieving, she spoke aloud in a fervent prayer, "Lord, please help me. I can't spend the rest of my life crying!" and her tears abruptly stopped. By the grace of God, she felt a supernatural calm settled over her and it remained.

"Blessed are those who mourn, for
they will be comforted" (Matt. 5:4, NIV).

Several nights later, Ellen was awakened after a vivid dream. She was walking on a dirt path, squinting against the brilliant sun that was stinging her eyes making it difficult to see what was ahead. The form of a young priest came into shape. She called out, "I know you!" Whistling a happy tune, the man stopped and turned around; it was her Joey, smiling that knowing, little smile that she had seen so many times before. His countenance pierced her heart and she felt his joy. He was a grown man. He was walking into heaven and he was happy to go.

"He has made everything beautiful
in its time. He has also set eternity in the
hearts of men; yet they cannot fathom
what God has done from beginning to
end" (Eccles. 3:11, NIV).

Life continued forward, and the next year, Donald was born. Bringing him home, Mom and Dad passed him from one set of loving arms to the next. The hollow place in their grieving hearts overflowed once again with the sweetness of new life. There was routine again in their lives as they cared for the new baby. As Donald grew, he became strongly attached to Dad. Donald kept a vigil near the front living room picture window, where he waited patiently for Dad to arrive home from work. Hearing the roar of big machinery, Donald would pull himself up to the windowsill, waving in excitement to see his dad's truck turning into the driveway.

When the other kids were at school, Donald could often be found perched on an overturned bucket or a stack of bricks, thoroughly entertained just watching Dad at his workbench. One day, Dad placed a small piece of wood he had cut from the end of a two-by-four board and a handful of nails beside Donald on the floor of the garage. Briefly instructing Donald how to hold a hammer, he left him to the job. Passing through the garage on her way to the back-yard clothesline, Mom paused in amazement. Donald had found a cast-off bottle cap and sat deep in concentration while he drove one nail after the other into the bottle cap flattening it as he went.

"What did you do?" Ellen asked him when he finished pounding. He smiled up at her, as she bent over to examine his work. In amazement, she counted twenty-four nails driven into that one small bottle cap and piece of wood. "How did you do that?" she asked. Proudly he beamed as he waved his hammer. Observing Donald's simple triumph overwhelmed his mother's heart. She could still experience happiness, despite her great loss. Soothed by the joy on his face, Ellen opened her arms and embrace him with deep and sincere gratitude to God for such a gift.

Ellen often wondered if all mothers found such contentment in watching their children grow. It did not occur to her to strive for any other occupation save for the one that she had. There was never a time that she felt she needed anything else to fulfill her. Believing strongly that raising her family was her calling, Ellen knew she would do her best with whatever God brought into her life and never question if she were up for the task. Her faith told her that God provided for all her needs and He would also make up to her children anything that she lacked.

My mother's faith continued to grow and so did her family. I was born the year following my sister Germaine. Several years later, the next blessing was expected to arrive over a Fourth of July weekend. Dad phoned home from the hospital that day, his voice thick and tight, to say that Mom was doing well, but the baby would not be coming home. Peter had been stillborn.

Several days later, my mother came home, retreating to her bedroom until she regained her strength. Though for a while the spark was not in her eyes when she smiled at us, the motions of her daily routine were soon reestablished. Mom kept private her personal struggle to forgive those involved in the circumstances surrounding her loss that day. She had overheard the nurse relay to her doctor that the surgeon who was called to consult on her difficult labor would not arrive until he finished his game of golf.

With her heart breaking, she labored knowing something was not right. Hours later, the surgeon finally arrived and after a brief examination, shook his head. Dispassionate, he told the nurse there was nothing he could do, and then he turned and walked out. She was left with the nurse and doctor to deliver Peter stillborn, though Mom had felt his movements just a few hours earlier. Her first and last act of love to Peter was to hand him back into the arms of his Heavenly Father.

> For it was you who formed my inward parts; you knit me together in my mother's womb. I praise you, for I am fearfully and wonderfully made. Wonderful are your works; that I know very well. My frame was not hidden from you, when I was being made in secret, intricately woven in the depths of the earth. Your eyes beheld my unformed substance. In your book were written all the days that were formed for me, when none of them as yet existed. (Ps. 139: 13, ESV)

To Mom's great delight, the next to be born was a bright, blue-eyed ray of sunshine, her treasured little red-head, Sharon. Soon we welcomed the last to be born, and forever her baby, Thomas. Just a few weeks later, Mom led her family up the aisle of the church to sit for a time in adoration before the Blessed Sacrament. It was the week before Easter. Holding her newborn infant on her lap, Mom took out her rosary and began to pray for each of her children. When she began her prayers for Joey, she closed her eyes and envisioned him sitting to the side of the altar looking just as he did when he was alive. Joey raised his arm, directing her gaze to Jesus in the Sacred Host displayed in the Monstrance. Mom understood with profound wisdom that Joey wanted any thoughts that she had of him to draw her eyes to Jesus. In her prayer, Mom felt very close to the sons who were no longer physically with her. She now sensed that there was a very thin veil separating them when she sat in God's presence in front of the Eucharist and she welcomed the ensuing peace.

A mother's mystical connection to her children may never be fully understood, but it is there nonetheless. I do not doubt there are safe places in our hearts—sanctuaries—to hold our deepest grief until we are able to face it. We ourselves must process our loss, yet in its complexity, it somehow begs to be kept private as well as be acknowledged by others. When moving from consolation to consolation, we may realize that we have marked our life from joy to tragedy and tragedy to joy, just as we would notch a child's growth on the frame of the bedroom door. Our faith shows evidence of its growth, just as a maturing child would, when the strength we have gained is used in turn to strengthen someone else.

"For just as the sufferings of Christ are ours in abundance so also our comfort is abundant through Christ" (2 Cor. 1:5, NASB).

*****

We were told that the conflict overseas was over, but in our world, it was far from finished. "Linda, it's time to let him go," Mom counseled the young wife of her eldest son Nicholas. "The medicine is not making him better." Nicky, an army staff sergeant recently returned from the Vietnam War, had little fight left to draw even a shallow breath. The once handsome father of three small children now lay in a veterans' hospital bed, barely recognizable to his loved ones. His body was filled with cancerous lymphoma. The treatments he had endured left his skin looking ashen and green against the stark white sheets.

Relinquishing her place beside her son, Mom left his grieving spouse in solitude to find her peace. Back in her room in the army hospital barracks, Mom dozed on and off while praying her rosary. Exhausted and with eyes closed, although not asleep, she envisioned a crucifix on the wall across the room. As she watched a scene begin to unfold in her mind, she concluded, "They are taking Jesus down off the cross." She then thought, "No. That is not right. Jesus had hair. This man doesn't have any hair. Yes, I see now. It is Jesus taking my son off that cross." Purposefully she rose from the bed and began to dress. Mom reached her hand out to grasp the doorknob when the phone began to ring. Without turning or stopping to answer, she continued out the door. She knew Nicky was gone.

Decades later while watching a television program, Mom saw a depiction of Jesus as He appeared to the young Lithuanian artist, Akiane Kramarik, in a heavenly vision. Astonished, she pointed to the image and said, "*That* is the Man! His likeness is astoundingly the same as the man I saw in the vision that day in the hospital. He was the one taking Nicky off that cross."

"I have been crucified with Christ and I no longer live, but Christ lives in me" (Gal. 2:20a, NIV).

Consolation from God becomes a gift beyond price when we face the hardships of life. My mother depended on her faith in making hard decisions as well as keeping the faith when decisions were made for her. Years later, when one of her daughters fell seriously ill, Mom wanted to go across the ocean to be with her but *discernment in prayer* held her back. Mom felt in her heart that if she went to take care of the grandchildren then her daughter would give up rather than fight for her life. After an interminable recovery, her daughter acknowledged that it might well have been the truth.

At the time, there was nothing that her sick daughter wanted more than to have her mother by her side. However, she found that in her mother's absence, God placed a treasure in her heart. Her daughter learned that while she felt she had no more control of her circumstance than a grain of sand when the waves of the ocean washed over the shore, *she* was safe in God's hands. Her daughter realized that even though the tide may determine if the sand was drawn back into the sea or carried high and dashed against the rocks, because God was with her, she had no reason to fear. Whether the sand was baked in the sun, chilled in the night, packed hard by feet that tread upon it or built into a castle by a passing child, it would remain sand. Resolute, she decided, that no matter what happened, she wanted to remain pliable to the will of God in her life.

It was a very bleak time for Mom when one of her sons lay succumbing to a severe illness in a hospital nearly three thousand miles away. When the doctor called recommending that she immediately come, she first prayed and then felt sure in her heart that she should wait. Trusting in God's timing and *offering up her pain* of separation, she waited for the Lord's prompting to tell her when she should go. At that same time, it happened that her son's closest friends were gathering around him at the hospital and encircled his bed in prayer. To the amazement of the doctors, her son recovered. As soon as she was able, Mom then made the trip to see him with her heart at peace. Together they celebrated the miracle with healing walks through butterfly sanctuaries and beautiful flower gardens abloom with new life.

Prayer was Mom's *shield against fear* the day she was notified that one of her daughters had been injured in a terrifying chainsaw accident. She prayed fervently, trusting that God's love and mercy would give her daughter courage and strength to pull through. Her daughter later related that while forced with a slow and painful convalescence, she began to feel God's love in a deeper way than ever before.

So close to death when the blade sliced through the skin of her neck, her daughter fully expected to open her eyes the next moment in heaven. Instead, she woke to an agonizing reality and a painful recovery. Given a new lease on life, yet grieving the loss of seeing her Savior face-to-face, her daughter began questioning everything until all her "whys" became silent. In her prayer, she came to realize the many ways that God was communicating His love to her. Surrendering her heart to God, she pledged to live her life ever aware of His Divine Will and found even more purpose in her life.

Mom knew what it was like to be awakened from a sound sleep to be told that her son had been in a dreadful car wreck. The shock of hearing his neck was broken did not divert her from sweeping up her rosary as she dashed out the door. Mom knew her rosary was a *weapon in spiritual warfare*, and she prayed in earnest, thanking God that her son was alive. As her son struggled through his recovery, Mom never wavered in her faith that God was doing a great work in his life.

> "Peace I leave with you; my peace I give to you. Not as the world gives do I give it to you. Do not let your hearts be troubled or afraid" (John 14:27, NABRE).

We gain a new perspective of our circumstance and of the world when viewing it through our faith and God's Word. Our pain becomes a refinery. It can turn even abject misery into purpose. We can see deeper truth by holding our thoughts up to the light of Christ in the Gospel. Unfailing in His faithfulness, God will turn what the enemy meant for our harm into the weapon used for our victory.

"Consider it all joy, my brothers, when you encounter various trials, for you know that the testing of your faith produces perseverance. And let perseverance be perfect, so that you may be perfect and complete, lacking in nothing" (James 1:2–4, NABRE).

THE HEALING JOURNEY BEGINS

It was difficult for me (the author) to leave the town where I was born because so much of my family was still there. I especially missed the closeness I enjoyed with my sisters. Looking through the church bulletin at our new parish, I saw an invitation to join a women's Bible study and decided to attend.

I was warmly welcomed when I arrived at the meeting. I was surprised at the depth of sharing while discussing the book of Ruth and the devotion Ruth showed to her mother-in-law Naomi (Ruth 1:16). The women gathered there were eager to share their insights and the many correlations they saw in their own relationships.

The conversation flowed passionately and the testaments to their faith convinced me that everyone had a story worth telling. I closely watched the crestfallen face of a young widowed mother, still grieving the loss of her husband. I saw her face brighten as those seated nearest her reached out to comfort her, offering words of encouragement and practical advice. Amazed at God's provision for her, I realized the importance of each one of us being there together.

Many of these women, like me, were transplants to the picturesque coastal town of Grand Haven, Michigan. I came to be in awe of the lovely women of all ages and various stages of their lives and began to see the infinite value of each one's story. The living Word of God was manifesting right in front of me as I watched the experienced wives and mothers of the group mentor the younger women gathered there in fellowship (Titus 2:3–5).

God knew what I would need and provided before I even arrived. When I thought of my large, loving family, I felt sad for women who struggle through life without sisters, or sisters in Christ. It made me want to find those who did not have the kind of support that surrounds me in the body of Christ and implore them to connect. We were not meant to walk our journey alone.

"Two are better than one, because they have a good reward for their toil. For if they fall, one will lift up his fellow. But woe to him who is alone when he falls and has not another to lift him up!" (Eccles. 4:9–10, ESV).

Being kept apart from one another weakens our power in Christ. We find solace and are blessed when we come together and magnify what God has done for us in our lives. It is a joy when we learn to recognize our Savior's voice and an honor when His Spirit prompts us to speak what we hear. At times our heart will pound, knowing He has something to say. Many times, we will not even be aware of what is happening until a word, timely spoken, is confirmed to be just what someone needed to hear.

When we are aware of the Holy Spirit's presence in us, we can see opportunities for blessing others wherever we go, even at times when all is not well in our own lives. When looking back on the path of my life, I realize that the shadows of darkness in the valleys make the mountains of victory stand out brilliantly in contrast.

Our God is the God of many chances. He is able to make a crooked path straight and help us reach our destination no matter how many detours along the way. Many times, I have allowed fear to sway or completely stop me. When frozen with indecision, I once believed that not making a decision would still be better than making a mistake. Healing prayer makes possible what before seemed impossible.

> "And we know that God causes all things to work together for good to those who love God, to those who are called according to His purpose" (Rom. 8:28, NASB).

SWEET SYMPHONY

A soul divided is a wasted thing.
Who's to gain if I can't live what I believe.
Time's a grain of sand that's slip-
ping through my hand
And all I can hold on to is
what I cannot see.
So sing in me, Your sweet symphony.
All that I need is a sim-
ple song and a melody
And words that can be a love
reflection of our harmony
So sweet to sing.
Prison walls of my own making
Contain the fears of my escaping.
I cannot hide, although I've tried.
My soul cannot be sated
but by the Voice that has cre-
ated this song in me.
This sweet symphony resounding in me
It's a simple song and a melody
That's longing to be a love reflec-
tion of our harmony
So sweet to sing.
(*Song by Eileen*)

In my healing prayer, I saw myself as a preschool age child, pacing the length of our front living room windows. I paused periodically to scan the road anticipating the return of my older brothers and sisters from school. I then drifted over to where my mother sat in the rocking chair nursing the baby. I lifted the long pink ribbon that dangled from the sleeve of her housedress. Wrapping it around my finger until it curled, I tickled my baby sister's soft cheek with its silky end. "Why don't you go outside and play for a while," Mom suggested. Dropping a kiss on my little sister's curly red head, I bounded off.

The early autumn sun was warm on my skin as I wandered outside and down the front path. Passing the beds of brightly colored petunias, I wrinkled my nose, their pungent odor making me sneeze. The extra length of the cast-off dress I had found on the floor of my big sisters' closet, dragged in the dirt behind me like the train of a storybook princess. A mirror would have revealed an image quite contrary to the blissful mental picture I held of myself at that moment. The only gauge of how beautiful I considered myself to be was measured in how deeply I felt I was loved. Circling the large willow tree, I twirled happily in the abundant folds of my beautiful, old, cast-off gown. I began singing with joyful abandon to someone I imagined to be just out of sight in front of me.

I innately trusted that my hopes and dreams were just waiting for me to arrive. Nevertheless, just as quickly as I noticed my happiness, it was shattered with the thought, "There's no one there." I looked up from my game, uncertain if the words were from someone actually speaking to me or if it were a trick of my mind. Either way, the one to whom I had been singing to felt completely real to me despite the voice trying to convince me otherwise.

I had been feeling the presence of someone *Ever Present*, who loved me unconditionally, who knew me and my desire to know Him. This incident exemplified to me how insidious the enemy can be in his attempt to separate us from the peace and presence of God. My childish joy shifted to uncertainty, then fear and confusion crept in. Pulling my attention away from God, I was no longer content to just be in the present. I began wondering, "Who was watching, what they were thinking about me and was I behaving appropriately."

A sea of faces plays on the landscape of my early childhood memories. Rewinding them now as if I hold a remote in my hand, I pause at a place where I feel uncharacteristically alone. I can only feel sorry for myself for a brief moment because a hero appears in the form of one of my siblings sweeping me up in their arms. Briefly pulling me close, they proceed to set me beside them on the piano bench and begin to guide my small fingers over the keys.

This is my place. I belong. I believe it. It did not matter in the least that the socks on my hands replaced mittens when a spare pair could not be found. It was not important that the clothes in the closet were community property. When arriving last to the boot-closet and finding the only galoshes left were two sizes too large, "make do" or "go without," were the obvious solutions.

The memories that are endearing are not a problem. However, I discovered the disturbing memories that the Lord called to mind in my healing prayer held opportunity for God to help me to grow and change. The daily events triggering emotions that brought me to tears, caused an overreaction or prevented me from moving forward in life, begged for transformation.

> "Come to me, all who labor and are heavy laden, and I will give you rest. Take my yoke upon you, and learn from me, for I am gentle and lowly in heart, and you will find rest for your souls. For my yoke is easy, and my burden is light" (Matt. 11:28–30, ESV).

The day I was scheduled for healing prayer, I began wondering where I should begin. My circumstances were not easy at the time, and it was maddening to me that I was unable to cope. I constantly felt worse than the situation warranted. When I arrived for my Transformation Prayer Ministry (TPM) appointment, I was already feeling helpless and frustrated. After beginning our healing prayer session, I became more agitated as a cascade of memories began to unfold. "What's happening?" asked Sharon, the woman trained in TPM.

I felt a part of me opening up, and a strong desire to be heard began to swell in my chest. With eyes closed, I clearly saw a memory of me as a four-year-old child perched on the edge of the kitchen counter. My thought was, "I can't see!" Sitting there alone, in the dim light of the florescent bulb that shined beneath the upper cabinet, I was feeling afraid of being caught while secretly pulling at the bandages that covered my eyes. I strained to get a look around the perforated patches I was forced to wear since having corrective surgery to straighten my crossed-eye. I felt like I was suffocating, like I could not breathe until I removed the dressing from my eyes.

That strong feeling was just an ordinary response of a small child who didn't fully understand the value of those bandages. Yet somehow the feeling of *helplessness* in not being able to see clearly and *frustration* at being kept in the dark had remained with me to adulthood. The beliefs became a stone in my foundational thinking. Although it no longer served me now, it still felt very real. The strong emotions that left me feeling helpless and frustrated in the past were resurfacing again in my adulthood when I did not see the reason behind someone's motives.

In situations that triggered similar strong emotion, I could easily convince myself that I could not see my way clearly and could not trust the motives of others. To protect myself, I had developed behaviors that resulted in a pattern of helplessness and frustration that was presently causing me pain. In prayer, I invited the Holy Spirit to reveal His truth in the memory and asked Jesus to remove any defenses I had developed. In that one prayer, God freed me from habitually taking offense, from unnecessary suspicion and from an exaggerated seriousness. My trust in others was restored and what seemed impossible for me before, now felt natural and easy.

"But thanks be to God! He gives us
the victory through our Lord Jesus Christ"
(1 Cor. 15:57, NIV).

Fortified by the relief I felt through TPM, I pursued another healing session. I had been unable to shake the pain from a conflict with someone, and I agonized that it was *entirely my fault.* I carried guilt on my shoulders like a security blanket, and it was an exhausting burden to bare. In my prayer, I asked Jesus what He wanted me to know about that strong feeling of guilt, and I became aware of another memory from my childhood.

A winding creek and woods ran the length of our deep backyard. The barn set back on the edge of the property begged for exploration. It had provided plenty of opportunities for my adolescent siblings and cousins to get into mischief before, and this day was no different. My older brother was our self-appointed chief, the younger four of us eager to follow along. We crept into the barn and peered through the slats that divided the entryway from my dad's large machinery. To our delight, we spied a mammoth blue elephant.

Our oldest sister and her high school friends had created the full-scale model elephant for the Monroe County Fair Parade. Constructed out of chicken wire and blue tissue paper flowers, the elephant float had been dropped off in the barn and still sat atop and anchored to the trailer, waiting to be dismantled.

In fear of being caught, we cautiously approached to investigate. The opening in the model elephant's side was barely detectable but once found, beckoned us to climb inside. I was the last one to squeeze in through the hole. After a moment of nudging those to the side of me so I would fit, I questioned our intent but was quickly hushed.

My brother solemnly announced we were about to hold a pow-wow in our new, secret hiding place.

The head of our small tribe, all of ten years old, brought out a small candle and matches from his pocket. I watched as my brother ignited the wick of the candle that he had balanced between his knees. Questioning our safety but not waiting for a reply, I scrambled to my knees and backed out the opening. A unified cry broke the stillness of the air when my quick movement dislodged the candle from its precarious position, setting the tissue paper ablaze. I jumped down from the trailer, my heart pounding as I ran toward the house. Throwing a look over my shoulder, I saw the others tear from the barn scattering across the lawn, fleeing in all directions.

Our older brother Dave heard the commotion and looked up from the car he was working on. Upon seeing the smoke coming from the barn window, he bolted from the garage with a fire extinguisher in his hands. Shouting for us to get Mom, he rushed into the barn and put out the flames moments before they spread to the hay stacked against the wall.

My shrill cry brought my brother Brian to the kitchen window and he came running, a dish towel still clutched in his hand. I cried pathetically while he hastily beat the smoldering tissue paper that had caught in my sandal. Smoke billowed from the windows of the barn and sirens soon filled the air. The flaming elephant had been engulfed, and when the firemen arrived, they doused the remains as well as the smoke charred rafters. Scared and mortified, yet all unharmed, we were called to line up against the house as the fire chief proceeded to sternly reprimand us on the dangers of playing with matches.

My healing prayer revealed that I often felt it was "all my fault" because the phrase was cemented in a brick of my foundational beliefs. I had proof enough that I had indeed caused the candle to fall and ignite the paper elephant. Yet in my prayer, besides removing my guilt, Jesus helped me to see things that I had not before. I saw the wisdom in leaving an obviously dangerous situation, and the power of our mother's prayer to enlist our angels' protection.

CHAPTER 4
Joy

"These things I have spoken to
you, that my joy may be in you,
and that your joy may be full."
—John 15:11 (NASB)

I felt a sense of order surrounded by my brothers and sisters. I had a concept of having my place in line, and it felt comfortable to me. However, as one of the middle kids, I was left in a kind of limbo as my older brothers and sisters began to graduate from high school and college and move on to having families of their own.

Each with their own interests, I could no longer tag along with the older kids because I was too little. I could not get away with what the little ones could because I was too big. I was often bated with the chant "Go play with someone your own age!" or "Go play with someone your own size!" Those comments depicted the kind of offhanded remarks that became a springboard for a once contented adolescent who only wanted to play, to jump with both feet into the confused world of a rebellious teenager who just wanted to fit in.

The solution to my predicament presented itself once I left the familiarity of my parochial grade school to attend the all-girl Catholic high school. As I walked into the first school dance, I was drawn to the guitar strains of REO Speed Wagon's "Ridin' the Storm Out" echoing in the hall. I moved through the crowd of unfamiliar faces, making my way across the floor of the gymnasium toward the stage area. I casually joined the girls gathered there in front of the band. We were soon dancing circles around each other and I realized I had never felt so free. In the short pause between songs, I met Anna and we became instant best friends.

By the end of the night, Anna and I made an agreement to meet at school on Monday outside the door of the freshman locker room. Our plan was simple. Get off the bus, check into homeroom, and walk out the back door of the school. Once we had made it that far, we walked as nonchalantly as we could across the back-parking lot. We held our breath as we ducked through a hole that someone had cut into the fence, our minds spinning trying to come up with a plausible excuse if we were caught. We felt an adrenalin rush as we approached the all-boys high school down the street. Rounding the corner of the parking lot, we spied a group of guys smoking cigarettes in their cars. Without saying a word, we headed in that direction picking up our pace.

Daily we came up with new ways to make the same mistakes. We paired perfectly, like drunk and disorderly or shame and regret. It was agony when we could not spend every waking moment together. The more the rules demanded of us, the more determined we became to find a way to escape their constraint. Eventually we would be made to pay the price. Those in authority thought that making us attend two different schools would curtail our shenanigans and we were separated. Our creativity was taken to new heights and we took up the gauntlet.

Before we even graduated, we were packed to leave home. We persuaded my older brother to let us come along when he moved to Colorado. We planned to find jobs and rent a room from my sister who already lived in Boulder. We were not a day on the road when the sickness began. I prayed the whole way there that I only had the flu or another bout of homesickness—the kind my cousins used to tease me about when I'd stay for sleepovers—but deep down I suspected that was not going to be the case.

When we finally arrived in Boulder, I tried to ignore the symptoms as best I could. Soon after, I found a job at a supermarket deli, and Anna and I found a house to rent. At work, my supervisor began to comment disapprovingly on my frequent trips to the restroom and questioned the tears that often threatened to spill from my eyes. It was obvious my flu-like symptoms were not going to go away. Flipping through the phone book, I found the address for a free health clinic. Arriving for the appointment, I walked through the door and felt a chill go up my spine that I would come to find had nothing to do with the air-conditioning or temperature.

After the brief examination, I sat stunned as the doctor announced that I was pregnant and asked when I would like to schedule an abortion all in the same breath. I wanted to be a mother for as long as I could remember and now, although only eighteen, I was going to have a baby. If need be, I would have left my own leg behind to escape with my child. The minute I was left alone in the room, I escaped silently down the hall without stopping at the scheduling desk. I didn't look back. When I called the baby's father back in Michigan to tell him the news, he said, "Then I guess we should get married." Naively, I agreed.

My dad arrived in Colorado before I could make plans to go back home. He repeatedly tried to persuade me to stay with my sisters, pleading with me not to return to Michigan to get married. He predicted in ten years and three kids later, I would be divorced. The harder my dad tried to convince me, the more stubborn I became. I had talked myself into believing the marriage would somehow work out. Returning to Michigan, I persisted in my plan, even attempting to get permission to be married in the Catholic Church.

Failing the compatibility test, the church in her wisdom counseled against the marriage. I would not fault my father's absence from the hasty courthouse ceremony. I was well aware of what he thought. Trying to silence a subtle ominous ticking I heard in my heart, I ignored the pain and learned to live with my decision. I would see in hindsight that I seemed to be a person who learned the hard way. Nothing tempers harder than grief.

> "I will give them a heart to know Me,
> for I am the Lord; and they will be My
> people, and I will be their God, for they
> will return to Me with their whole heart"
> (Jer. 24:7, NASB).

Just as my father had predicted ten years passed and the disintegration of my marriage was obvious to me and could no longer be denied. In a last-ditch attempt to reconnect, my husband and I planned a short trip together. I had made the flight arrangements when suddenly I was struck by a surge of terror. What if I got on that plane and it crashed? I would wake to find myself separated forever from everyone that I loved.

In a panic, I called my older sister in search of some reassurance. I knew full well that my past, irresponsible behavior had gone against everything that I was raised to believe. There had been so much pain, deception, and betrayal that I could not live with myself anymore. The excruciating mental agony was driving me back to the roots of my Christian faith in search of forgiveness and hope. My sister suggested that I might feel better if I called her parish priest to talk about my difficulties. I hesitated with good reason.

Shortly after my first two daughters were born, I had attempted to return to my Catholic roots. I had them baptized and attended Mass on Sundays, but I still did not feel connected to the church. My unhappy married life eventually drove me to the confessional to seek some kind of guidance and reassurance. However, what I did not expect was for this elderly priest to instruct me in the catechism. I had little understanding of what receiving the sacraments really meant and felt condemned. Still miserable, I left the confessional crushed and confused and resolved I would not be back. Just like a child who does not understand or accept their parents' rules, I pouted in self-pity, having expected consolation not correction.

Now, I was moved by my sister's gentle invitation, and she assured me her priest was relatable and was sure talking with him would help me. What did I have to lose? I was only going to talk to him. I was surprised when he walked into the room with the stole of official priestly duty around his neck, and I regrettably realized that he presumed I was there for confession.

Unwilling to clarify why I had come, I went along as he led with the opening prayer of reconciliation. Having Catholic school indoctrination into the faith I knew that the sacrament called for a contrite heart. So would fear alone count, I wondered. I had been instructed in the faith and the IHM Sisters at my high school made their best attempt to get it from my head to my heart, but those years had been a joke to me. I smirked at the fleeting thought that I should add that to my list of sins.

However, nothing could have prepared me for what was about to happen. With halting effort trying to recall the process, I began, "Forgive me, Father, for I have sinned . . ." As the words left my lips, a sob was drawn from the depths of my heart. Abruptly and uncontrollably, I began to weep. Handing me the box of tissues from the table between us, Father listened. All the things that I had hidden, the destruction that brought me to this point in my life, became blindingly recognizable as sin.

The things I had said and done, things I knew had caused others pain, began to play before my eyes. I revisited all the places I had gone searching in vain for the illusive "something" and the repercussions that left me walking away even more hurt and confused than before. Astonished,

I began to realize how many innocent bystanders had been caught up in the web of my past schemes. I stared mournfully into the dark bottomless void I had been desperately attempting, though unable, to fill.

As I hopelessly cried out my pain, Father sat quietly and said nothing. I began yearning to feel the safety and comfort I had felt when I was young. I wanted to look at my reflection in the mirror and see the eyes I had seen before a tortured man's hand destroyed the innocence of a confused and frightened child. I felt talons of unforgiveness gripping my heart, and I wanted it to let me go. I began to despise the slippery slope of instant gratification and self-obsession and the places where it led me. I had been hurt and I had falsely believed I no longer cared what happened. In reality, I was deeply sorrowful for the hurt I had caused. I saw who I had become and recoiled at my own image. In an unexpected vision, what would be the first of many, the mirror reflecting my image shattered. I felt my world was spinning out of control and I grasped for the moral compass I had lost, desperate that it would point me in any direction away from the one where I was headed.

"Now faith is the assurance of things hoped for, the conviction of things not seen" (Heb. 11:1, NASB).

Like a shaft of light piercing a dark room, it dawned on me that I had taken my first step of faith. I felt the draw of an unknown path beaconing me. I could turn around! Struggling to remain in the present moment, I fixed my eyes on the crucifix hanging on the wall behind Father, and I felt hope seeping through the cracks of my broken heart and personality. I welcomed it. I dared to believe that what was transpiring was real. I stopped struggling with the fear and my panic ceased.

As my emotions calmed and my tears slowly subsided, Father inquired, "Is there anything else?" My breath caught in my throat and I sniffed, doubting he even understood a word I had said. I shook my head. He then said, "Then I absolve you of all of your sins in the Name of the Father, and the Son, and the Holy Spirit." All of my sins? I wondered. Had I heard him correctly? The truth of what had just happened sank into my heart. I was forgiven. Then Jesus, the Jesus who I had only known in paintings and poetry, suddenly became astonishingly real to me.

I vividly sensed that I had somehow been transported through space and time and found myself at the foot of the Cross on Calvary. He had taken my sin and nailed it to a tree. It was done. No one could take that away from me. I could both be a sinner and still be saved! I was forgiven, but not because of any merit that I had or because I deserved it; not even because I was officially acquitted by those I had offended. I was forgiven because I was loved. Jesus loves me because I am His. I knew this was a debt that I could not repay, and it would forever inspire an offering of love, gratitude and adoration on my part. His grace had hit its mark. Amazed, I realized I no longer felt the fear of getting on an airplane. The concern had simply vanished.

For my penance, the priest in his wisdom and in the custom of the Catholic Church sent me to sit in the quiet of God's love. I walked across the parking lot and into the empty church. Sliding into a pew, I settled in front of the statue of the Blessed Mother. As the afternoon sun streamed through the stained-glass window and fell on the image of her face, I tried to relate to the Queen of Heaven. Feeling much like a small, humbled child, shyly embarrassed at what had occurred, my heart overflowed with an unfamiliar love. It was love like the ebb and flow of a tide with a power of its own.

Before the Mother of God's beautiful image, I closed my eyes. I suddenly had the impression that Our Lady really was there with me, stepping down from the pedestal and beckoning me to come to her. After a moment of hesitancy, I did. I opened my heart and raced unashamedly into the arms of the Mother of Jesus as she welcomed me back into the fold of her Son. Imbued with a sensation of profound peace, I felt her gently guide me to my place within the Body of Christ once again.

> "When Jesus saw his mother there, and the disciple whom he loved standing nearby, he said to her, 'Woman,-here is your son,' and to the disciple, 'Here is your mother.' From that time on, this disciple took her into his home" (John 19:26–27, NIV).

I was not sure what to do with the newfound hope and the excitement I was feeling for my faith. It was clear to me from the song of thanksgiving and praise pouring from my heart that I wanted a way to express my gratitude for the generous mercy I had been shown. Again, at my sister's invitation, I joined her at her parish church. She explained we would be attending a charismatic prayer meeting where I would find support and encouragement in my walk with Christ. The songs were uplifting, and I felt welcomed as if they had known me for years. It was all new and wonderful and strange at the same time. I felt like a distant observer when their prayers turned into unintelligible sounds and melodies that I later learned was called "praying in tongues."

I would discover that although I felt somewhat out of place, God wanted to prove to me that He knew I was there and wanted me to know it. I listened as the others shared Scriptures, words they sensed were from the Lord, answers to prayers and how they saw God working in their lives. I began to hunger to hear God speak to me in that same way.

Later that night, I sat at home alone in my room. Sitting on the edge of the bed staring at my folded hands, I began, "Lord, I . . ." and then I stopped when I realized I had no idea what to say. Rocking gently back and forth, I thought about my life and tried to figure out how this was supposed to work. Where should I begin? What was expected? How was I supposed to act now? What should I do? I knew my marriage was broken. What would happen to my children if my marriage could not be repaired? How would we live? Where would we go? How would I provide for them? I could come up with no answers and struggled to suppress my tears. Just then the phone began to ring, startling me from my rumination.

I answered and the voice on the other end explained, "This is Pam from the prayer meeting tonight. I hope you don't mind, but I called your sister and got your phone number. I know it's late to be calling, but the Lord has just laid it on my heart to call you right away and give you the scripture Matthew 6:25–34. Do you have a Bible? Would you write this down? I just feel it is something He really wants you to know."

Mystified, I listened to all she said then thanked her. I hung up the phone wondering what was happening. I dug beneath the clutter at the bottom of my closet to find the Bible my mom had given me when I first left home. Holding it to my chest, I climbed back onto the bed. Flipping through the pages, I found the passage she referred to and I began to read it aloud.

> "Therefore I tell you, do not be anxious about your life, what you will eat or what you will drink, nor about your body, what you will put on. Is not life more than food, and the body more than clothing? Look at the birds of the air: they neither sow nor reap nor gather into barns, and yet your heavenly Father feeds them. Are you not of more value than they?" (Matt. 6:25–26, ESV)

In stunned silence, I stared at the passage. How can this be? I turned my eyes toward heaven but felt myself slipping to the floor and onto my knees. I had encountered the Living Word. The Body of Christ was alive. I heard the voice of God as if He had spoken directly to me and by His grace I recognized His voice. How was this possible? I had been listening to these stories my whole life. Why could I hear Him speak now? I held my Bible close and whispered, "Thank you."

> "The LORD appeared to him from afar, saying, 'I have loved you with an everlasting love; Therefore, I have drawn you with loving kindness'" (Jer. 31:3, NASB).

God drew me to Him, deeper and deeper, as I began to hear His whisper through others, and through the Word again and again. I had learned several guitar chords while in high school, and I decided one night to play an old hymn I found tucked in my Bible. I soon found myself changing the words and the order of the familiar chords trying to express what was in my heart. After tucking the girls into bed at night, I turned on a fan, as I often did, to muffle any noise that would disturb them. Sitting in the farthest corner of the living room, I strummed softly recording my journey back to Jesus in song.

Shortly after my encounter with the Living Word, it was announced at church that there was an upcoming "Life in the Spirit" seminar. Its purpose was to bring people into a deeper experience of the Holy Spirit and His gifts and to create a clear understanding of the power of His Word. Excited to participate in the renewal in the Catholic

Church, I attended the weekly meetings anticipating the stories of how others saw God working in their lives.

> "But the Helper, the Holy Spirit,
> whom the Father will send in my name,
> he will teach you all things and bring to
> your remembrance all that I have said to
> you" (John 14:26, NASB).

I was eager to see God's presence in my own life the way those who were sharing their stories did. I felt like a toddler let loose on the playground, happy to be there but not sure what to do. After the final session, we were invited to be prayed over by the leaders of our group. I sat on the steps of the altar with two of my very close friends who I had persuaded to come to the seminar with me. We were invited to pray for a release of the spiritual gifts: wisdom, understanding, counsel, fortitude, knowledge, piety and fear (awe) of the Lord (Isa. 11:2–3). Without warning, an indescribable joy began bubbling up simultaneously in all three of us. Trying unsuccessfully to remain solemn and dignified, we succumbed to the joy. Refreshing waves of tears and contagious laughter washed over us leaving a childlike happiness in its wake.

> "You did not choose Me but I chose
> you, and appointed you that you would go
> and bear fruit, and that your fruit would
> remain, so that whatever you ask of the

Father in My Name He may give to you"
(John 15:16, NASB).

The more fervently I sought my faith the more evident it became that I had little control over the outcome of my deteriorating marriage. There was nothing more devastating to me at the time than feeling the call to holiness with no known way to achieve it. I was being drawn to the sacredness of love while being torn apart by the consequences of the dreadful choices I had made in the past.

I knew that I was required to love but did not have a clue where to begin. The mistakes I had made, though now under the Blood of Jesus, still had consequences that I could not fix on my own. Upon discovering I was expecting our fourth child, I felt indescribable happiness. It was a bitter irony that when sharing the news with my children's father, he permanently walked away.

The last pretenses of my marriage finally crumbled. We were not able to stay in our home, and the children and I carried our possessions, each in our own plastic bin that easily stacked in guest rooms, living rooms or basements, wherever space was found for us. We moved each month back and forth for a year to the homes of friends and family whenever they could take us. Holding fast to what I experienced the day of my confession, I found comfort in knowing God was with me and would take care of us, no matter how painful our daily reality.

Growing up, I had been handed my faith on a silver platter. Previously, I had intellectual knowledge of Jesus. It was not until the day of my sincere confession that I experienced a personal love encounter with God and my faith became my own. That changed everything because it began to change me. I had stepped outside and gotten myself wet in a shower of His mercy and forgiveness. I now had irrefutable proof of God's love because I had experienced it. I knew God loved me, that I was accepted, forgiven and not alone.

My daughters had all been born easily and quickly and without complication or intervention, and I expected the same for my fourth child. I was looking forward to having a natural birth and my first experience with a midwife. When stepping on the scale for my forty-week check-up at the women's hospital, I began to change my mind. I had gained seventy-five pounds and I did not want to remain pregnant for one more day in fear of gaining a single ounce more.

I would not listen to any objections when I requested labor be induced. I had my best friend and coach Anna already there with me. In fact, Anna had been with me at every appointment throughout my pregnancy, aiding and abetting when we stopped for ice cream on the way home from each doctor visit. The weight gain was no mystery. I knew I had been trying to offset the pain of bringing my child into a broken family. I craved the instant gratification that one thousand calories and fifty grams of fat would momentarily give.

I was already two centimeters dilated, lived forty-five minutes from the hospital, and there was a predicted snowstorm on its way. My midwife reluctantly agreed to induce labor. I called my two sisters to pack up my daughters and come to the hospital; I was being admitted to the maternity ward.

It was several hours before the contractions began with the help of Pitocin, and it was not long before it was time to push. The fact that there was no father present in the room was offset with the love of my three young daughters, two sisters, a niece, and my very best friend.

The midwife was soon announcing I had a son. My heart sang, "A boy? A boy! A boy . . . Thank you, Lord!" I quickly asked Saint Joseph, foster father of Jesus, to pray for him and take him under his watchful care. I then named my son Ethan Joseph, meaning "strong, firm" and "to add, increase." I could not wait to take my baby home and lose myself in the wonderful familiar feeling of caring for a precious newborn.

After a yearlong search for affordable subsidized housing, I finally secured a home for my children. I could see the hand of God orchestrating everything in minute detail. An unknown caller rang to inform me of a house that was soon to be for sale just down the street from my mom. It met the criteria for subsidized financing and the loan was approved in a fraction of the time anticipated. I knew I was being handed a gift. My dream of staying at home with my kids soon became a reality when my brothers transformed the two-and-a-half-car garage into a beautiful childcare center. Enrollment swelled to capacity right along with a list for children not yet even born. In gratitude for how God was providing for us, I scheduled time to go away on retreat with friends to the Franciscan University in Steubenville, Ohio. My youngest, Ethan, was now three years old, and I was ready for some time away to spend in reflection.

The weekend passed all too quickly. I felt uplifted, blessed, and refreshed as I stood amid the small group gathered to pray over us individually during the final session. When our prayer was concluded, I was nearly skipping as I headed back to my seat. Feeling a touch on my arm, I stopped and turned to find one of the Franciscan sisters had caught up to me.

Sister paused a moment before explaining, "The Lord gave me a word for you as we prayed, but I wanted to give it in private. May I share it with you?"

"Yes, of course!" I assured her. "Please do!"

"You will need to discern for yourself what it means, but the Lord told me to tell you, 'Do not be afraid to give me your Isaac,'" she recounted seriously.

Slightly taken aback, I thanked her and proceeded to my seat with considerably less enthusiasm. I continued to turn the phrase over in my mind as I made my way over to the chapel to wait with the others for the priests to arrive to hear our confessions. The soothing, gentle music drew me close to the altar. I found a seat beneath a beautiful banner of Saint Francis and Saint Clare; the one with hands raised, the other, her hands clasped in ecstasy before the Blessed Sacrament exposed in the tabernacle. I contemplated the phrase I had been given from Genesis 22 and the possible meaning of what I had been told. What did I need to surrender? Was there something precious to me that I needed to entrust to God? Having no answer, I tucked the word I had been given into my heart, completely oblivious to how soon it would become frighteningly clear.

CHAPTER 5
Peace

"Then the peace of God that surpasses
all understanding will guard your
hearts and minds in Christ Jesus."
—Philippians 4:7 (NABRE)

I thought it was just an occupational hazard. Kids will have colds and infections, and in a day care, illness spreads quickly despite the best disinfecting efforts. The substitute sitter arrived at the day care, and I composed a list of instructions for her. After asking my daughter Leah to come with me to help, I packed up my sick three-year-old son and headed to the car. Buckling Ethan into his car seat, I bristled at yet another of his all-too-often sick doctor visits.

When finally shown to the examination room, I paced as we waited for our pediatrician to come in. When the doctor entered the room, I explained Ethan had a slight fever that would come and go, poor appetite, and listlessness. I also pointed out a strange splattering of red dots on his leg and abdomen and a bruise that would not go away. I was thirty-five years old and ran a day care out of my home, seeing children coming down with an illness was no stranger to me nor the doctor, but he certainly seemed to be indicating that he was taking my explanation seriously, too seriously for what I thought was a general illness. I expected the typical instructions for another round of antibiotics and salves and nodded impatiently at his observations. I looked down at my watch and thought of the fast approaching, often chaotic, pick-up hour at the day care.

As he probed my son's liver, the doctor said, "Mother, this is serious. Very, very, serious." Pulling me aside, he grasped my arm and looked into my eyes. I stood motionless while he quietly and compassionately told me he suspected my son had leukemia. I was told to take him immediately to the children's hospital. He clasped my hand gently then turned and left the room to make the arrangements.

In utter shock, I looked down at Ethan. He strained to climb into my arms. "Home!" he demanded. Kissing the top of his head, I picked him up and passed him to my daughter Leah. I asked her to take him to wait in the car. I drew a deep breath as chills ran through my body, and I began to shake. I knew that I could not fall apart, and my mind fought with the dark phantom of fear that was gripping me. My mind screamed, "Wait. No! No, there's been some mistake! This can't be happening!"

I looked around the room and struggled to pull myself together. I found myself in a vacuum where time raced and stood still all at once. Somehow, I found myself back in the car with a handful of the doctor's orders. Unable to explain my distress, I avoided eye contact with Leah and handing her my cell phone told her to call my sister Chris and have her meet me at home immediately.

Chris and I both pulled into my circle driveway at the same time. Gesturing for Leah to take her brother inside, I ran to my sister's car. Grasping her hand as she opened the door, I pulled her up the front porch steps, through the door and down the hall. Closing the bathroom door behind us, I gasped for air as if I had been forcefully punched in the stomach. "He said Ethan has leukemia." Collapsing into her arms, we both wordlessly sobbed.

Nothing else needed to be said. Our thoughts went immediately to the loss of our brother to lymphoma when we were young, and more recently, our dad, both having succumbed to cancer. The storm passed as quickly as it had begun and releasing my grip on her arms, I turned to the sink. Splashing icy cold water on my face and then wetting a cloth, I determinedly scrubbed away the bitter tears, mentally preparing for what lies ahead.

I gathered Ethan's favorite things and I kissed my daughters goodbye, assuring them they would hear from me soon. When we arrived at the hospital, Ethan was quickly admitted, and they immediately began the preparations for surgery. As soon as the blood tests were completed, he was to be taken down to the operating room where they would insert a catheter into his chest to begin chemotherapy.

Sitting with Ethan in his room waiting for the gurney to arrive, my mind focused on the date. It was April 2, the ten-year anniversary day of my dad's death from cancer. Was this a coincidence? In the last days before Dad passed away, I remember him struggling to say that he was offering up his suffering to God with hope and praying his kids and grandkids would be spared such an end. I disregarded what he had said at the time, but now I silently prayed it was somehow true.

> "Rejoice in hope, be patient in tribu-
> lation, be constant in prayer" (Rom. 12:12,
> ESV).

My sister Mary Beth soon arrived at the hospital and promised I would not need to go through this alone. She pledged to be by my side, no matter what happened. It was exactly what I needed to hear. Having her there with me shouldering my burden lightened the weight I felt bearing down on me. Once shown to the waiting room, we began the vigil of prayer that would establish a habit for the heart-breaking years to come. Counting rosary beads instead of minutes, together we prayed.

We began by thanking God for all the events that led us up to this moment where Ethan could be helped. We prayed for the doctors, nurses, and staff. We prayed over the medication and instruments that they would use. We implored the help and intercession of the saints, the assistance of the angels, and for the Blessed Mother to pray for us. We prayed that those in our family who had passed away before us would pray for us now.

> "First of all, then, I urge that supplica-
> tions, prayers, intercessions, and thanksgiv-
> ings be made for all people" (1 Tim. 2:1, ESV).

Giving no room to the inauspicious thoughts fighting for a foothold, we began a litany of thanksgiving for all that God had done for us in the past and for all that He promised us in His Word. We spoke blessing into Ethan's body and bound the enemy from interfering. We united our prayers with all the Masses being said around the world, surrendering our own will.

We prayed to receive all unclaimed blessings. We prayed as well for all those around us in the waiting room. We prayed for those suffering without knowing God's comfort. Praying for those who suffered alone, we asked that He be with them in their hour of need. We encircled everyone who had no one to pray for them and especially for those who were in the process of making difficult decisions.

> "Do not be anxious about anything, but in everything by prayer and supplication with thanksgiving let your requests be made known to God. And the peace of God, which surpasses all understanding, will guard your hearts and your minds in Christ Jesus" (Phil. 4:6–7, ESV).

My fingers seeking out and gripping each rosary bead, I trusted. Vaguely aware of my surroundings, I wondered how my breath continued, steady and even, given the circumstances. Hours later, I finally heard Ethan's name called from the desk and was asked to follow the nurse. I had to consciously slow my steps as my heart propelled me toward my son like the undeniable draw of a magnet. I was familiar with the waking process after a child had been given anesthesia. Ethan had tubes placed in his ears and two eye surgeries to correct a cross-eye in the past. However, nothing could prepare me for the scene I encountered. I would learn that what I was unable to process at the time would remain stored in my heart until another day. In fact, it would resurface ten years in the future, on a spring afternoon, very close to the anniversary date, whether welcome or not.

> "Do not be afraid, for I am with you.
> Don't be discouraged, for I am your God.
> I will strengthen you and help you. I will
> hold you up with my victorious right
> hand" (Isa. 41:10, NLT).

I knew the grief would not overtake me if I could keep my mind on the blessings. Seeing the good around us was a lifeline, and it quickly became an irreplaceable discipline. I consciously counted every grace coming through each heart-rending experience. It was evident that we were still very blessed. I saw blessings in the efficiency of the caring staff when my son awoke from surgery and in my brothers arriving to join me in the recovery room, their very presence giving me strength. I sought God's goodness with diligence. I was determined to be aware of and acknowledge every help that He sent.

Soon Ethan, heavily medicated, was resting back in his room. My family left for the night with the promise of continued prayer. I carefully moved the rocking chair as close to Ethan's bed as I could and cautiously sat beside him. Finally left alone with my little boy, I looked frantically around the room at the beeping machines and IVs attached to his body and the reality brutally struck my heart. Gazing down at his small hands folded tightly over his baby blanket, I felt the panic begin to rise and I could no longer contain my groan of looming despair.

> "Though He slay me, yet will I trust Him. Even so, I will defend my own ways before Him" (Job 13:15, NKJV).

I heard my own cry in my heart, "Lord! It is not my word, but your Word that is at stake if he does not survive this!" I had read the Scriptures. I knew its promises. "By His stripes we are healed" (Isa. 53:5). "He sent His Word and healed them" (Ps. 107:20). I stared intently at the pastel balloons printed on Ethan's baby blanket snuggly tucked around him by the nurse before she left the room. I watched his chest rise and fall with his labored breath. Utter anguish tore me apart.

I didn't attempt to stop the rivers of tears streaming from my eyes. Willing my spirit to submit to God, I whispered, "But if you should take him . . . still . . ." I resolved, "Still, I will praise You." In direct response, I sensed His comforting words, "Even so it is not the will of your Father which is in heaven, that one of these little ones should perish" (Matt. 18:14). I gasped at the understanding. I did not need to convince God of an unjust pain. We were in this together. He was on our side. His Word was truth and

I would trust Him. With a deep sigh, I closed my eyes, allowing God's grace to soothe and strengthen me. Where He would take me, He was able to keep me.

My thoughts drifted to my girls being cared for by my niece. My heart ached that we were separated. It brought back a memory of when my daughters were very young. Driving down a bumpy country road, I had been gripped with fear as I suddenly imagined that if I somehow lost control of the car, I would be responsible for their harm. I remember tightening my grip on the steering wheel and glancing back in the mirror at their joyful, carefree faces. Remembering the Guardian Angel prayer from my youth, I had begun to fervently pray, "Angel of God, my Guardian dear; to whom God's love commits me here. Be ever this day at my side, to light, to guard, to rule and guide. Amen."

Much to my surprise then, I felt a reassuring pressure on my shoulder, and I found myself declaring out loud, "They are first yours, Lord. You have placed them in my care, yet it is You who ultimately care for them. I am doing my best and I know you are with me." A noticeable change occurred, and I breathed a sigh of relief.

In the same way, I now felt the obsessing fear and heartache loosen its hold on me as I began thanking the Lord for allowing me the privilege of being part of my daughters' lives. Peace began to wash over me. I acknowledged God's faithfulness was the same yesterday, today, and forever, and I knew that would never change. I mentally left my girls in the hands of God and those who were caring for them. Relieved of the anxiety, I was able to peacefully turn my attention to my son.

"Let us then with confidence draw
near to the throne of grace that we may
receive mercy and find grace to help in
time of need" (Heb. 4:16, ESV).

That first night we spent in the hospital, I experienced
an outpouring of grace that became a filter through which
every experience would be viewed. I realized that for all the
faith I had placed in God, faith that He heard my prayers
and faith that He would spare my son's life, I had a choice.
I needed to decide right then whether I could and would
go on in that same faith if Ethan did not survive. I came to
the conclusion that faith was not dependent on any feeling, circumstance, or outcome. It was a choice. I chose to
believe and trust. I had no idea then how that trust would
be tested to its very limits.

"But when Jesus heard it, he answered
him, saying, 'Fear not: believe only, and
she shall be made whole'" (Luke 8:50,
KJV).

There are many defining moments in our lives. Be
it a serendipitous encounter or a divine appointment, we
remember each detail and it forever changes us. When I
received Ethan's diagnosis and the treatment plan, it was as
if I saw a tsunami heading toward us and my feet were frozen to the ground, unable to move. It was a primitive inner
battle to succumb to the inevitable and quietly slip under

the waves, or to grab Ethan and run knowing full well it was unlikely we would escape.

Perched on the edge of Ethan's bed, I forced my mind to concentrate on the sketches his doctor was drawing. He described what they hoped to accomplish with the proposed treatment and what we should expect. I was overwhelmed at the length of the projected schedule. I politely thanked the doctor for his help and turned to comfort Ethan.

When the doctor, interns, and nurses cleared the room and Ethan lay quietly watching a video, I slipped into the adjoining bathroom and softly closed the door. My mind was spinning with details. The pain and suffering Ethan would endure were made more real by the memory of our loved ones already lost to cancer. My thoughts were of my girls fearfully waiting at home, the parents of the children in my day care who counted on me, the bills waiting to be paid week by week. How could we survive this? How could I take care of Ethan and still provide for my family?

I felt grief and hopelessness wash over me, fear and worry draining my strength; I sagged against the wall and slid down to the floor struggling to stifle the sobs that were being wrenched from my stomach. Crouched there I cried out to God to help me. In response, I felt a subtle gentle pressure on my shoulder. "It's in the mail." At once calm, I rose back to my feet. The angelic reminder had broken through my oppressive thoughts. I looked ridiculously at my face in the mirror above the sink. Sharply I inhaled. "What?"

My thoughts seemed to answer as quickly as I thought the question.

"Would you be this distressed if you knew help was in the mail?"

"No," I thought in response, "I would be in there comforting and caring for my son and trusting God for the rest!"

Again, I sensed, "It's in the mail." Ringing as true as any promissory note, I tucked the words in my heart. I thanked my guardian angel for the reminder of God's provision, and I confidently turned the knob on the door and resumed my post at Ethan's side.

Jesus, I trust You became my anthem as I sought to keep my equilibrium and strength as Ethan pressed through each of his treatments. Three long days of tests and procedures were followed by three sleepless nights. I kept my vigil by Ethan's side. I tried to anticipate his every need, to somehow lessen the discomfort and pain, to absorb what was happening to him, and somehow explain and then distract him in the process. A parade of unfamiliar doctors, interns, nurses, and aides caused apprehension in Ethan and disrupted any privacy and rest. The questions and observations were endless as they ordered continual testing, often into the night. I felt as though we were caught up in a surreal movie, and it was all beyond my control to make it stop.

"Fear is useless, what is needed is
TRUST" (Mark 5:36b, TLB).

Nodding off in the twilight of sleep, I was aware of Ethan's breathing as I cradled him beside me in his bed.

I had the distinct impression, as happened many times before, that someone had entered the room. I felt as if I had opened my eyes, yet what I saw convinced me it was an inner vision. At the foot of the bed, surrounded by a soft glowing light, stood the saints whose words I read with enthusiasm when I first fell in love with Jesus. My gaze fell first on Saint Francis of Assisi and then Saint Clare, my companions in private peaceful meadows during meditation and prayer. The third I thought must be, because of his armor, Saint George the legendary dragon slayer. Then there stood the very familiar Saint Thérèse of Lisieux, my namesake in baptism, who smiled shyly. The fifth, dressed in a nun's habit as well, I did not recognize. I sensed her saying, "I am Margaret Mary" (Apostle to the Devotion to the Sacred Heart of Jesus). I mentally shook myself fully awake and carefully sat up. There was no one and nothing there except the dim light and a soft beeping from the IV monitors. However, the panic that had gripped me was gone. I turned away from the seduction of fear and acknowledged that I had nothing to dread for I was not alone.

> "Beloved, do not be surprised at the fiery ordeal among you, which comes upon you for your testing, as though some strange thing were happening to you; but to the degree that you share the sufferings of Christ, keep on rejoicing, so that also at the revelation of His glory you may rejoice with exultation." (1 Pet. 4:12–13, NASB)

News of Ethan's illness soon reached those who knew us. As never before, I began to see Jesus walking and talking through His people in the Body of Christ. Very weary after two weeks of caring for Ethan in the hospital yet unwilling to leave his side, I yearned for someone's shoulder to rest on. Late that evening, a nurse walked in and handed me a large brown bag with the logo of my favorite restaurant in town. "I think your husband left this for you at the desk," she said. Instead of explaining that I was a single mom, I just smiled. It would be one of many times that I would recognize God sending others to show me that I was not alone, that He was providing in His way for our every need. With each bite of the fresh, delicious dinner, my soul was nourished, and strength began to course through my exhausted body.

I reached out to touch my son's hot forehead and became more aware than ever of the all-surpassing love that God the Father has for each of His children. It was more than just a thought; it was an irrefutable knowing. I was beginning to see our circumstances in the light of the Gospel. There were endless hours of waiting at my disposal, and I prayed God would use the time to show me more.

> "And these signs will accompany those who believe: in my name they will cast out demons; they will speak in new tongues; they will pick up serpents with their hands; and if they drink any deadly poison, it will not hurt them; they will

lay their hands on the sick, and they will recover" (Mark 16:17–18, NIV).

So much of what was happening was out of my control but there was much to do on my internal battleground. In my Bible group, I had learned I had certain rights in Christ. What did that mean? What did it look like? If I knew how it worked, how would it help? How should I pray my way through what we were going through? I felt I needed to understand the principles of effective prayer and committed to searching the Word of God until I did.

I could accept the fact that we would be in the hospital until we were released. However, would I accept the Word and maintain an attitude of hope, even joy, at the same time? (James 1:2–4) Despite the pain and heartache, could I declare out loud that God would use it for our good and for His glory? (Rom. 8:28) Although I had documented proof that this serious illness was real, could I stay strong and believe that "by His stripes" my son is healed? (Isa. 53:5) I wanted to curl up in my prayer and cry out that I could not continue to watch my son suffer, and chose instead to stand and declare, "I can do all things through Him who strengthens me" (Phil. 4:13). My solemn prayer was quickly becoming, "Lord, I can't. You can. You promised!"

After two weeks, we were finally released and returned home to a restless night. In the predawn hours, I sat on the floor of my unnaturally quiet, vacant day care. Folded in my lap were all the scriptures I had scribbled and collected throughout the years. I knew the words. They had spoken to me before. I believed they were Truth. They had been tucked in assorted drawers, books, and bags throughout the house. Now, with gentle deliberation, I opened each one like a priceless gift and read it aloud.

Then setting them aside, with purpose, I stood and opened my daycare storage cabinets. I began hastily rifling through the shelves until I had stacks of colored paper and markers strewn across the carpet. Kneeling on the floor, I wrote out each scripture using the boldest colors on the brightest paper in my most confident handwriting. Completing the task, I proceeded to laminate each one using clear contact paper.

Gathering up the laminated scriptures, I walked through the house securing them to the kitchen cabinet doors, both inside and out, on the refrigerator, dishwasher, on mirrors above the bathroom sinks, on the windows and doors, above our beds, and on the walls around every turn.

Every surface I saw or touched now spoke encouragement and truth. I knew if I were left alone with only my thoughts, they would threaten me with hopelessness and despair. My own thoughts could not be trusted. I needed to quote God's promises until His Word formed my thinking. I needed to see the truth everywhere I turned. I now had accessible instructions at all times on how to think and what to do.

"These commandments that I give you today are to be on your hearts. Impress them on your children. Talk about them when you sit at home and when you

> walk along the road, when you lie down
> and when you get up. Tie them as sym-
> bols on your hands and bind them on
> your foreheads. Write them on the door-
> frames of your houses and on your gates."
> (Deut. 6:6–9, NIV)

At first it seemed uncomfortable and hypocritical to speak aloud according to the truth in God's Word, especially when it appears contradictory to the reality we were experiencing. It was more difficult still when in 1998, after his first year of chemotherapy, we were told that Ethan had suffered a spinal relapse. His treatment would continue for another year. The news drove me deeper into the Word. From cover to cover, I read the Bible highlighting the words that spoke to me. I discovered we were caught up in a spiritual battle that was even bigger than what we were seeing manifest before us. Although our circumstances felt overwhelming, I was assured I had nothing to fear because my God was, still is, and always would be on His throne.

> "For we wrestle not against flesh and
> blood, but against principalities, against
> powers, against the rulers of the darkness
> of this world, against spiritual wickedness
> in high places" (Eph. 6:12, KJV).

I also began to understand a villainous methodology that was keeping us entrenched in the medical system, as each medication given needed others to counter its side effects. It may be hard for outsiders looking in to imagine what would possess a parent to follow blindly a harmful protocol without being given explanations of options. There was no counsel on where to gain an education about the disease, a reason for its cause, or any other ways to aid in helping my child to better heal. However, follow I did, in fear of consequences and in ignorance. Not only was I asked to bring my child to the hospital to receive injurious chemical therapy, I was now being instructed to administer the treatments at home between hospital visits and it was becoming more than I could stomach.

The instruction to bring him back to the hospital immediately if his temperature rose over 101 degrees was taken very seriously. Even with our prayers, an elevated temperature occurred with regularity. Too often, after his treatment, I would wake to his feverish cries at 3:00 a.m. and I could not wait until later that morning nor deny the need for medical intervention. The gravity of the side effects from the drugs he was taking made it necessary to stop what we were doing immediately. It didn't matter if it happened in the middle of the night, on my daughter's First Communion day or Christmas Eve. Consistently, these fevers would upset our lives and the lives of others who would step in to assist my family during Ethan's hospital stays.

It became my habit to pray over Ethan in the night as he lay laboring under the caustic medications. I filled the space in my mind and every inch of the room with the goodness of God. With my hands over his head, I quietly proclaimed blessings to come upon him, go before him, and follow him always. Lovingly speaking to Ethan's ravaged cells, I encouraged every muscle, bone, tissue, organ, cell, and system to perform to the perfection for which it was created through his Savior Jesus Christ. The language of the Spirit, praying in tongues, was the melody Ethan took into his sleep. "Sleep tight in the Sacred Heart of Jesus," I whispered my deepest desire when he finally stilled, "with everyone we love and everyone who loves us!"

> "With every prayer and petition, pray
> at all times in the Spirit, and to this end
> be alert, with all perseverance and requests
> for all the saints" (Eph. 6:18, NET).

When my hands slid from Ethan's head as exhausted sleep overtook me, I soon awoke again to his soft whimper. "Mommy, please do what you're supposed to be doing," he urged, breathing heavily, voice shaking and hoarse. Reaching for my hand, he placed it back on his forehead. How many ways did it help? Would we ever know?

A thousand times, I placed my trust in God and became more aware of how He was leading me even deeper into trust. I would often hear the words of Father George Kosicki, who spent his life spreading the message of Divine Mercy, encouraging me, "Trust. Then *trust even more.*" When no longer able to ignore our dire financial situation, those words gave me strength to dial each creditor to work out a manageable payment plan to keep up with my growing debt.

"But as it is written: 'What eye has not seen, and ear has not heard, and what has not entered the human heart, what God has prepared for those who love him,'" (1 Cor. 2:9, NABRE).

At night when everyone else was asleep, I sat focused on the flickering flame of the burning candle at my kitchen table. I prayed, my hands resting on the stack of unpaid bills and deductibles. I began to recite my Litany of Trust, conceding that God could do what I could not. I realized that prayer was a priceless gift, even in my restless, sleepless hours because I saw our needs being miraculously met over and over again. I had been given so much help. I filled the hours of waiting and watching for Ethan's healing to manifest by praying for those who had helped us, for those I knew needed help and for the intentions of all those who came to mind.

In thanksgiving, I prayed for those who sat beside me for endless hours in waiting rooms, for those sending food, those caring for my other children while we were in the hospital. I prayed for the day-care moms who stepped in to watch each other's children in hope that my day care could soon reopen. I asked for special blessings for those whom God inspired to stop in to check on us, for repairs made to our roof after a severe storm, for the Good Samaritan who fixed my flat tire and the thoughtful one who mowed the lawn while we were in the hospital. I prayed for the generous anonymous one who left money in my screen door the very day I was in such need of groceries, leaving with it a cheerful note wishing us a good day with a simple request to just "pray it forward."

God had given me more than I felt I could handle, and I was learning to rely on Him for everything by inviting Him into every aspect of our lives. When the temptation to become embittered grew strong, God's grace directed me back to my faith. Hidden under the illusion of self-sufficiency, He unmasked my pride. He illuminated my fears lurking in the darkest corners of my heart, and I conceded to the necessary process of struggle and surrender.

> "Beloved, I pray that all may go well with you and that you may be in good health, even as your soul prospers" (3 John 1:2, ESV).

When I allowed my mind to wander into the murky water of doubt, it threatened my peace and only magnified my problems. When I could no longer emotionally bear it, my exhausted mind shrieked, "Lord, what more do You want? What more can I do?" Prayer drew its own answer and God inspired me to desire His solution as He bid, "Rest in Me" (Matt. 11:28). The state of my soul began to take precedent over my comfort. I decided the burden of each painful obstacle in my path would become a stone I would use to build an altar to His omnipotence and glory. Relinquishing control of the plan I had for Ethan's healing, I asked God to show me what He was doing through our crucible of confinement.

My heart was again torn the day we arrived at the hospital to begin another year of chemotherapy. It was so close to the date that his treatment should have been over. There would now be a change to Ethan's protocol. We followed the nurse from the infusion playroom, where Ethan had been trying to play with other children, despite the limitations and the unpleasant effects of their chemical IVs. We were asked to wait in the examination room until his doctor could come and discuss the results of Ethan's tests. Once again, we would not be going anywhere anytime soon.

Entering the room, Ethan stopped short and picked up a prescription pad and pen he saw lying on the table. The nurse and I both looked down to admire his four-year-old scribble. To our amazement, my little boy had plainly scrawled the word *F U N* across the pad. It was the first word he had ever written. At the pitiful irony, I raised my head; I sadly smiled at the nurse who turned away quickly but not before I saw the tears forming in her eyes.

> "Rejoice always, pray without ceasing, give thanks in all circumstances; for this is the will of God in Christ Jesus for you" (1 Thess. 5:16–18, ESV).

The hospital became my battlefield and my sanctuary, my prayer closet, and my mission field. Keeping God's Word close I became aware of Him moving all around us, especially in my own heart. For every disappointment, delay, or painful procedure Ethan endured, God was quick to console us with images of His love. The Holy Spirit repeatedly brought to mind Scriptures that illustrated His provision for all of us.

As the parent of a child in such desperate need, there was a necessary single mindedness that overcame me. Still it did not lessen the pain of separation I felt for my daughters who were left in the care of others and not their own mother. Tempted with guilt, I prayed for consolation and Jesus arrived for me in the loving image of the Good Shepherd (Ps. 23). I was reminded that God was there for me *and* for my children. Suddenly, I did not want for anything more than what I had.

The Good Shepherd beckoned me to lie down in green pastures beside restful waters and He restored my soul. Even in our dark valley, His rod and staff were guiding and comforting me. Though I felt battle worn, drained, and empty, Jesus led me to the table He prepared before me in the sight of my enemies. Renewing my strength, He anointed my weary head with oil. His mercy and goodness followed me, and I would dwell in His presence forever. No longer able to be with my daughters and mother them as I desired, I would rely on the grace of God coming from the power of His Word to console me. From all that I lacked flowed rivers of more than enough.

It was imperative to me that I know the truth of who I was in Jesus when confronted daily with the battle in my mind. In the beginning, pure determination kept me reading, memorizing, and meditating on God's Word. I wanted to crowd out my own thoughts with the sheer magnitude of God's words. However, soon His thoughts, His words became my own thoughts and a resting place and refuge where I could feel God's presence. Alone with my son in the dark of night when I thought the pain of his suffering would kill me, the blatant lies of the enemy that sought to destroy my peace became easily recognizable as being completely contradictory to God's Word and, therefore, easier to disregard. I bravely chose God's truth over the lies.

> "Submit yourselves, then to God.
> Resist the devil, and he will flee from you"
> (James 4:7).

I would not die but live to tell the marvelous deeds of God (Ps. 118:17). Fear was useless. What was needed is trust (Luke 8:50). I could do all things through Christ who strengthens me (Phil. 4:13). If we endure, we shall also reign with Him (2 Tim. 2:12). He has borne our grief and carried our sorrow. By His stripes, we are healed (Isa. 53:3). For God hath not given me a spirit of fear but of power, love, and a sound mind (2 Tim. 1:7).

> But do not ignore this one fact, beloved, that with the Lord one day is like a thousand years and a thousand years like one day. The Lord does not delay his promise, as some regard "delay," but he is patient with you, not wishing that any should perish but that all should come to repentance (2 Pet. 3:8, NABRE).

I could not rise in the morning to begin my day until I had God's Word in my spirit and any tears sternly arrested. I stood to face the day with the knowledge that God is love and I am loved (1 John 4:8). I nourished myself with the truth that He is compassionate and gracious; slow to anger, abounding in love and faithfulness (Exod. 34:7). Preparing to drive us to our destination each day, I confidently belted us in the truth of His promises, for He cannot lie (Num. 23:19). Stepping through the hospital doors I fixed my eyes on the Lord, with Him at my right side, I would not be shaken (Ps. 16:8).

> He answered, "Love the Lord your
> God with all your heart and with all your
> soul and with all your strength and with
> all your mind" (Luke 10:27a, NIV).

The chaos of my world propelled me to the godly order I found in Scripture. I was learning that while God's Word was in fact changing the reality around me, it was also creating a new challenge inside of me. Once my thoughts about our circumstances were in line with God's Word, His second greatest command, to *love your neighbor as yourself*, could not be ignored. I did not want an opportunity for introspection but now with nothing but time on my hands, the command stubbornly persisted.

> "By this everyone will know that you
> are my disciples, if you love one another"
> (John 13:35, NIV)

I was grateful to see God's hand in our circumstances, and I was unable to resist His correction and instruction. I wanted more of God's light to be reflected in me for others to see. I needed to be open to where He was leading me. As the Holy Spirit illuminated His timely command to "love your neighbor as yourself" (Mark 12:31), I recognized my difficulty in doing so. I welcomed what He was doing in me and trusted what He was able to do through me. I accepted God's forgiveness and love and I loved Him with all my heart, but *did I and was I able* to love myself?

God began a healing work in me by showing me that the thoughts and words I used to criticize myself, would clearly be recognized as demeaning, if I heard them spoken aloud to someone else. The Lord wanted me to know that the words I directed at myself were not harmless, and it grieved Him. *He* did not condemn my imperfections, but by my own words, *I* did (Rom. 2:1).

> "But now, O LORD, you are our Father; we are the clay, and you are our potter; we are all the work of your hand."
> (Isa. 64:8, ESV)

I wanted to understand the importance of having an open heart for Jesus, and I was signed up for a difficult and accelerated course. If God wanted to show me why it was important for me to have compassion and mercy for myself to truly love others, then I needed to learn to listen. I was not going to be taught, however, surrounded by those I found easy to love or in a comfortable living situation.

I would learn in circumstances that made my skin crawl and my heartbreak. Lessons would be delivered by perfect strangers who walked into our lives, disrupting our peace, day and night. Life's tutors would hand over assignments that would violate our privacy and inflict grievous injury to my child. Tests would be given, many with dire consequences as a result. However, I would find the answers I needed hidden in Scriptures that once read, continued to speak, the words unable to be forgotten.

When the Lord first called to me, found me, and drew me back to Him, He did it with love. He showed me undying love, undeserved, unsolicited, and unexpected. I wanted to learn to do the same. Knowing that Jesus *is* love, I knew everything I would do with love would bring me closer to Him. I knew my very ability to love was God's gift, generously given (Matt. 7:7).

Like a small child, I developed a desire to grow up to be more like my Heavenly Father. I could no longer delude myself and claim to love Him yet continue to dance to my own tune. God had plainly spelled out the meaning of His words. There was no room for error or personal interpretation. Jesus clearly said, "If you love Me, you will keep My commands" (John 14:15).

> "Love is patient, love is kind. It does not envy, it does not boast, it is not proud. It does not dishonor others, it is not self-seeking, it is not easily angered, it keeps no record of wrongs. Love does not delight in evil but rejoices

with the truth. It always protects, always trusts, always hopes, always perseveres" (1 Cor. 13:4-7, NIV).

CHAPTER 6
Patience

"O, Lord my God, I cried out
to you and you healed me."
—Psalm 30:3 (NKJV)

Unpredictable hospitalizations and interminable waiting provided ample opportunities for unresolved hurts to be triggered. As a result, my emotions were rising like rambunctious moviegoers attempting to get my attention and force their way through the door, as if my prayer time were a blockbuster showing on opening night. During my TPM healing prayer sessions, I discovered that any belief I formed that was lie-based would lead me to behave in unstable ways.

At a time in my past when I could not cope with a traumatic experience, I developed patterns of thinking that were no longer helping me. In fact, they hindered my life in many ways. In my healing prayer, I was freed from the thoughts that were not based in God's truth, and He healed the pain, which had been producing destructive and dramatic reactions to experiences in the present.

After experiencing TPM prayer and learning to better identify God's truth, I began to recognize similar suffering in others around me. I wanted them to experience the relief that I had found in my healing prayer. I began to pray that I could see past the smoke and mirrors, the illusions that the enemy was using to create fear, those that kept me bound to so many of my detrimental behaviors.

I realized I could not expect to effectively encourage others to overcome their fears without first having evicted my own. Contemplating my emotions as they arose, I took them to prayer and revisited the memories wherever they led me, *this time* in the light of Jesus. I continued to pray with a TPM minister whenever I could. Returning to memories that had previously felt cleared and places I had felt relief before, I was surprised a deeper belief could be unearthed. I began to understand the need for persistence in prayer.

My first healing experience through TPM dealt with my *fear* and *pain* as a four-year-old when I had corrective eye surgery. Returning to that same memory at another time, I realized I had also formed beliefs that I was *abandoned* and that *something was wrong* with me. As Jesus showed me truth about another aspect of my experience, and the truth about me, I felt relief. Asking, "Jesus, what do you want me to know about this (feeling/ belief)?" I could hear His answer more clearly each time I asked.

Sometimes the answer would come through a pertinent thought or Scripture, other times a feeling of peace would come over me. Often, I would see the memory in a new light. I recognized the voice as the same I heard when

I read the Scriptures. It was the same voice. It drew me to Jesus and caused me to want to know Him more. Of course, it is possible, like Saul on the road to Damascus, to hear the Lord without first really knowing Him at all.

> "My sheep hear My voice, and I know them, and they follow Me" (John 10:27, NKJV).

When we experience hardship, disappointment, pain, and suffering, we are not alone. Whether we feel His presence or not, God is always with us. During my TPM prayer, I became aware that there is nothing that can separate us from His love. He is here to show the *way* when we are lost. He is here to forgive, cleanse, and change us so that we can live a life without bitterness and regret. He is here for us in our most innocent mistakes to everyday disappointments, and even our most incomprehensible traumas. Faithfully, He frees us from the binds that entrench us in darkness and His healing fills us with His light.

> "These things I have spoken to you, so that in Me you may have peace. In the world you will have tribulation, but take courage; I have overcome the world" (John 16:33, NKJV)

Each burden I gave to God, He replaced with a gift. Each healing prayer left growing evidence of my changing heart. I was surprised when dealing with an unreasonable person, the gift of *understanding* left me more empathetic and willing to consider other's views. When faced with making a difficult decision, I found I had *knowledge* to know how to proceed. Having been comforted myself, I found ready *counsel* to comfort a grieving friend or stranger.

The most wonderful kind of love is falling in love with Jesus. Time in His presence softens our hard edges making it possible to become close and engaged with those in our lives without the barriers that often keep us at a distance. It can feel impossible to continue in a relationship that is filled with fear, loneliness, anger, and misunderstanding. However, when we are healed of our wounded emotions, it becomes possible and even enjoyable to build our relationships. Jesus, our Healer, desires for all of us to walk in freedom and is eager to help us. I cannot imagine my life today if I had not been led to TPM and been given the grace that helped me to change.

> "But it is the spirit in a man, the breath of the Almighty that gives him understanding. It is not only the old who are wise, not only the aged who understand what is right. Therefore, I say: 'Listen to me; I too will tell you what I know'" (Job 32:8, NASB)

My unfortunate motto for much of my life had been "call for help first." When problems arose, I looked for someone else to provide the solution. Spiritually, however, my shortsighted method was like passing over the owner's manual and asking the advice of a five-year-old to fix my problem. I may get a quick answer, but it's unlikely to be the best idea. There were no shortcuts to fixing my life. I needed to reconnect with the One who had the answers. Although I wanted concise, easy-to-follow directions that resulted in my desired outcome with a written guarantee, God's plan was not going to be all that predictable or comfortable.

> "I keep asking that the God of our Lord Jesus Christ, the glorious Father, may give you the Spirit of wisdom and revelation, so that you may know Him better" (Eph. 1:17, NIV).

God was leading me on a journey that would require my full participation. To my surprise, the rewards were endless. As I encountered unexpected trials and came face-to-face with my fears, I would ultimately come face-to-face with Wisdom. I discovered God actually wanted to teach me something with every experience that came my way— the good, the bad, and the ugly. Because I had made so many disastrous mistakes in the past, I felt my interior navigation system was broken. What I had not yet fully realized was that I had nothing to fear because Jesus was with me to lead the way.

> "Before I was afflicted I went astray, but now I obey your word. You are good

and what you do is good, teach me your decrees" (Ps. 119:67–68, NIV).

Before I began healing prayer, I formed a pattern in my hidden life where I would helplessly shriek in dismay at the uselessness of emotions while careening wildly on a manic rollercoaster of feelings. I did not understand what possible use the tide of emotions could be to me or to God. Although my behaviors began to change as I immersed myself in Scripture, an internal fire still burned as I struggled to get my emotions in alignment with the Word of God.

In *40 Days to a Joy-Filled Life*, based on Philippians 4:8, Tommy Newberry describes our emotions as a thermometer gauging the state of our thought life. I realized then that I did not need to correct my emotions, but that I needed to use them as an indicator of how well my thoughts reflected God's words for my life. If I was experiencing peace and joy, then my thoughts were dwelling on the goodness and blessings in my life. If I were experiencing sadness, frustration, and unrest, then I would be reminded to monitor my thoughts and revise them accordingly to God's instruction. Clearing lie-based beliefs through TPM healing prayer calmed my emotional responses and helped me to begin to renew my mind.

> "Finally, brethren, whatsoever things are true, whatsoever things are honest, whatsoever things are just, whatsoever things are pure, whatsoever things are lovely, whatsoever things are of good report; if there be any

virtue, and if there be any praise, think on
these things" (Phil. 4:8, KJV)

God promises we are never alone, as His very name
Emanuel "*God with us*" depicts. So why then do we feel so
alone, especially in times of stress and crisis? It is the darkness that distorts the truth and the deception that clouds
our emotions and keeps us immobilized. I had never experienced the enemy's tactics more noticeably than when I
wrestled with my fear of losing my son. Trusting in man to
find a solution to his illness became folly when not understanding what God was trying to tell me first. Our fears
are blinding. They offer no solution, yet we let them lead
us to make disastrous decisions that could be avoided if we
would heed and follow the whispers in our hearts instead
of the voices in our heads. Patiently God leads us, and with
patience, we learn to follow.

"By your endurance you will gain
your lives" (Luke 21:19, NASB).

Ethan's doctor explained to me that if there continued
to be leukemia cells present after another round of chemotherapy, the best chance for Ethan's survival would be
a bone marrow transplant. The search for a donor began
with the most obvious possibilities as Ethan's sisters and I
had our blood samples drawn to see if any of us would be
a match. Once again, through God's miraculous provision,
two of his sisters were perfect bone marrow matches. This
was not the norm and was a blessed relief.

"Even when we are too weak to have any faith left, He remains faithful to us. And He will always carry out his promises to us" (2 Tim. 2:13-15, TLB)

The snow had been steadily falling, and we were under a winter advisory the morning of Ethan's first radiation treatment. The packed snow crunched beneath the tires announcing my brother Donald's arrival as he pulled into the driveway at 4:30 a.m. to drive us to the hospital. Again, and again I thanked him, and thanked God that we had someone to help us. I sent up a silent prayer for all those who did not. Ethan's bag was packed with every comfort that could be taken with us—his favorite toys, books, movies, snacks, and everything that he might want while waiting for his radiation treatment. We were bringing everything I could think of that we would need if this daily treatment turned into an overnight stay. We were preparing for the bone marrow transplant with two weeks of daily radiation, and a snowstorm was not going to change the plan.

Although Ethan's radiation treatment was over quickly, the process of sedating him with anesthesia and waking him up was not. Late in the afternoon, we began our distressingly slow trek toward home. I cradled Ethan's head, sitting as close to him as I could despite the confines of his car seat. As I held him close, the scent of anesthesia rose from his lips with his weak cry and filled my nostrils. As he suddenly retched, I prayed silently that we could go faster, counting the minutes aloud for Ethan until we would be home.

Seeing a car slide into the ditch on the expressway ahead of us, my heart sank as I realized we were slowing down. I knew the disbelief showed on my face when Donald pulled off to the side of the road intending to help. Turning to me, he said, "I'm sorry. All I can think of is that could be one of your girls stuck in the snow. I have to help. It will be all right." Caught up in my own world, I struggled to nod my head, all the while devastated that it would delay Ethan's relief for even a moment.

I kept silent, finding it hard to breathe but knowing it was the right thing to do. Soon Donald was freeing the girl's car door from the piles of snow and leading her back to the road through the high drifts. Stomping her feet and brushing the snow off her legs, the grateful young girl settled into our car, vigorously rubbing her hands together. Her teeth chattered as she described her destination that would take us nearly an hour out of our way.

I forced myself to think beyond my own son's suffering to her plight and the concern of her parents waiting for her to arrive home. I clung to God's promised provision and tried to embrace the gentle urging to turn from myself, my desires, to the needs of others. My heart pounding, I began to thank God that we were here to help, that my own girls were warm and safe, that I had another opportunity to trust . . . even more.

My prayer of gratitude to God for the blessings of my family helped to distract the thoughts of worry. I remembered all the times this brother's voice, through his words of wisdom, had encouraged me to focus on my blessings instead of the struggles. I recalled when my oldest daughter was quite small, and without having enough change for the laundromat, I stopped by Mom's house to use her washing machine. Arriving and complaining loudly, I struggled with the car seat, diaper bag, laundry basket, and pregnant belly. My brother, Donald, fairly flew out of the front door, swooping up the laundry while listening to my troubles. With a wry smile he replied, "Yeah, but are you going to let it ruin your day?" Touché. We are given our teachers, and all our life lessons to prepare us for what lies ahead.

"He is like a tree planted by water, that sends out its roots by the stream, and does not fear when heat comes, for its leaves remain green, and is not anxious in the year of drought, for it does not cease to bear fruit" (Jer. 17:8, ESV).

We were admitted to the hospital for Ethan's bone marrow transplant just after Christmas. The long weeks away from my girls were anguish for me. I took great comfort knowing they were cared for by their "other mother," my sister Sherri. She had always been my extra set of arms when my children were growing up. There were too many times to count when she would sweep in like Mary Poppins and save the day for my kids and for me. I knew they were in good hands with my extended family and our family of friends.

My heart still ached for us to be together again. While Ethan rested, I filled the hours immersed deep in the Scriptures as I sat curled up at Ethan's feet, the morphine keeping him oblivious to the confines of our bleak surroundings. The constant drone of the massive filtration system in the ceiling numbed my mind to the world outside our walls. I counted on God's Word to be the light that was missing from our dreary room when the daylight struggled to reach us from around the concrete structure outside our solitary window.

I craved silence more than distraction and began methodically working my way through the Bible seeking any peaceful place He would lead me. Yearning for God's consolation, I paused at each verse and each chapter's end asking God to show me what He wanted me to know. Highlighting the words that spoke to me, I followed the trail of the Father's plan for my salvation. The stories I read came alive. Having nowhere else to go, I sat at the well with Jesus. There, laying bare my heart, He revealed the places in me that I had not yet surrendered.

When I began to lament the weeks confined to a hospital room, I adopted King David's posture in the Psalms, likewise pressing my downcast soul to praise God. Our hospital room became a cathedral of praise to God as I sang loudly to Him every moment that my mind was not unavoidably engaged elsewhere. There was no room for doubt and no other alternative than trust. I began to sense the Holy Spirit instructing me, giving me insight simultaneously as the doctors spoke. Listening for God's voice became a new reality for me.

"Come and see what God has done,
His awesome deeds for us!" (Ps. 66:5, NIV)

The scripture taped to the door of our quarantined bone morrow transplant room proclaimed to all who entered that they had just crossed a mysterious portal of miracles. When coming into our room, the staff and visitors saw the contradiction. It was heart-rending to see Ethan lying blanched and motionless against the brightly floral sheets I had brought from home, so noticeably out of place in our gray sterile room. However, they would not leave without the chance to stand in agreement with the awesome things we knew our God was doing for us. Prison or sanctuary, I needed to choose. By standing on His Word, I chose. Every moment of every day, I chose life.

"For since in the wisdom of God, the world through its wisdom did not know Him, God was pleased through the foolishness of what was preached to save those who believe" (1 Cor. 1:21, NIV).

I would only notice that another day had passed when the night shift nurse arrived. Once Ethan's medications were administered and his blood work completed, she left, quietly closing the door behind her. I sat and watched until Ethan's glassy eyes finally closed. His breathing slowed to an even rhythm. His soft whimpering stilled, and I then slipped cautiously onto my cot beside his bed.

This was the time of night my heart's sorrow welled up inside of me. I realized I had this one fleeting moment, alone in the dark, to let the trauma of what we were experiencing rise to my face. I silenced my anguished moan in my hand before it could pass through my lips, and I gazed up at the words I had taped on the wall above my head. "The Angel of the Lord encamps around those who fear Him and rescues them" (Ps. 34:7, NASB). I evenly drew in my breath, stilling my racing heart and then pronouncing each word slowly, deliberately ordering fear to leave the room and God's promise to descend around us like a cloud cover in the night.

ARMY OF LIGHT

One single cry split the night
as one shining knight flies
through the night on a perilous flight,
his sword by his side, ready to fight.
Swift as the wind, the prayer
that carries him over begins
And swells as a chorus joins in and the
armies divide, darkness and light.
What will you do, have you courage to carry you through?
This Army of Light cannot lose. But now
you must choose. What will you do?
On the front lines, the battle is
on; you can hold your ground
clothed in the Armor of God. The
trumpets will sound the victory won.
Belted in Truth, the Breastplate
of Justice is covering you. His

Helmet of Salvation and Faith as
your Shield, the enemy yields.
What will you do, have you courage to carry you through?
This Army of Light cannot lose. But
now you must choose. The Strength of
the Sword is the Word of the Lord.
(Song by Eileen)

After days of radiation, tests, and treatment, the actual bone marrow transplant day was hardly remarkable. Ethan's doctor came and sat on the floor where we were quietly playing and administered to Ethan an IV containing my daughter's bone marrow stem cells. As the days passed, the drugs used to suppress my son's immune system kept us confined to Ethan's small room. Each day the nurses came in to tell me which side effects should be expected. Their looks were often dubious and sympathetic when I would thank them for sharing their information, then, in turn, declare we were trusting in the Lord and believed that Ethan would not be adversely affected.

"And when they drink deadly poison,
it will not hurt them at all; they will place
their hands on sick people and they will
get well" (Mark 16:18b, NIV).

Ethan's weakness had not dampened his indomitable spirit. To compensate for the discomfort of the dreaded sterile baths and the regular changing of his Broviac bandage, Ethan and I designed rewards for getting them behind us for another day. Charts made with colorful construction paper and stickers counted off the days and portrayed adventures awaiting us once the countdown was completed and we were set free.

We drew pictures of ourselves in hot air balloons escaping from the hospital and flying high over the city to find our way home. We taped our dreams and goals among the dozens of scriptures scattered across the walls. We checked off the days on the calendar each night. We circled the earliest recorded date that anyone had ever gone home from a bone marrow transplant. Then we subtracted a day confident that we could break the record.

"I can do all things through Christ
who strengthens me" (Phil. 4:13, NKJV).

It had been two weeks and the only time I left Ethan's side was to shower while he slept. We were addicted to our schedule. I awoke each morning at 5:00 a.m. conditioned for years by my day-care schedule. I took out the weights and jump rope I had brought with me and worked out any doubts of God's victory before the morning nurse checked in with us.

One morning my sister Mary Beth and a friend, who was also one of the moms whose sons attended my day-care, arrived unexpectedly. I was pleasantly surprised at their visit until within minutes they announced that I was to go outside for a walk. Not given a moment to express my objections, I reluctantly allowed my friend to lead me away while Mary Beth distracted Ethan with a gift she had brought him. Exiting to the parking structure, the first blast of cold air stunned me as the automatic doors parted. Grateful yet distracted with concern for Ethan, I walked along beside my friend as we made our way downtown, trying to acclimate myself to my sudden freedom.

I slipped into the first bookstore we came to and began combing the children's bookshelves with the intent to find anything that would help Ethan to understand and cope with what he was going through. Stopping me in my frantic search, my friend compassionately counseled, "Eileen, it will be okay. You need to take this time to breathe. We should go back outside and walk so you can get some fresh air and sunshine!" In the tone of her voice, I heard her many years of experience as a school counselor, but it was the eyes of a sympathetic mother that met mine over the bookshelf. My look clearly communicated my anxiousness to return to Ethan and she refrained from saying anything more. I hastily purchased my selections and we returned to the hospital straightaway.

Our prayers were answered when Ethan came through his bone marrow transplant without the complication of graft-versus-host disease. He was released on the date we had envisioned earlier that month. Before we had even walked out the hospital doors, I began planning the grandest celebration I could think of for Ethan while at the same time cautiously holding my breath.

Saint Maria Faustina Kowalska was to be canonized on April 30, 2000. Pope John Paul II was to formally declare the Sunday following Easter to be the Feast of Divine

Mercy. My sister, Mary Beth, invited me to go with her on a weekend retreat to celebrate the special occasion. The Retreat Center was an off-the-grid property in the Upper Peninsula. There was no question it made me nervous to be so far away from Ethan. However, convinced that for the short time I was away Ethan's needs would be taken care of, I agreed. Mary Beth had been with me through every medical treatment that Ethan had undergone for three years. There was nothing she could ask that I would not do.

Among all the things I was grateful to her for, I was quick to remember the day Ethan lay sedated after a difficult spinal tap. I was staring miserably across the room to where Mary Beth sat in the corner, praying her rosary. I asked her then how it was possible for her to continue to come to the hospital and stay with us all the while watching what Ethan was going through. I wanted to know how she could sit and wait for countless hours that turned into years without ever complaining, without ever letting us simply continue alone, on our own.

The procedure had not gone well that day. The scar tissue, from so many repeated aspiration traumas to his spine, made it impossible for the nurse to puncture the site again. The force of her attempt to extract the fluid shook the treatment table beneath him and made Ethan cry out in pain. Demanding the nurse immediately stop, I sent Mary Beth running for the nurse practitioner that was overseeing Ethan's care that day. I know I could not have managed or even coped without my sister.

Mary Beth simply told me then that God had asked her to stay by my side and she could not have done otherwise. She knew in her heart it was God's will she be with us. Mary Beth was devoted to the teachings of Saint Faustina and Divine Mercy; to ask for God's mercy, be merciful, and completely trust in Jesus. Though Mary Beth had shared Sister Faustina's prayers and teachings with me often, it was seeing it lived out in my sister's life that instilled in me the desire to know more.

"For no word from God will ever fail"
(Luke 1:37).

We arrived in Paradise, Michigan for our retreat and our cabins were assigned. I felt honored that I would be staying in a small hermitage named after and dedicated to Sister Faustina. Late in the evening, I entered the small cabin and silently sent up a prayer of thanksgiving for the person who had come in earlier and stoked the fire. Every corner of the one-room cabin was filled with welcoming warmth against the biting northern Michigan chill. I could feel God's presence and comfort as I climbed into my sleeping bag. Zipping it up quickly, I pulled it snugly beneath my chin and began my night prayer.

I rolled each bead of my rosary across my fingers, reciting Saint Faustina's chaplet of Divine Mercy praying, "Eternal Father, I offer to You the Body, Blood, Soul and Divinity of Your Dearly Beloved Son our Lord Jesus Christ; in atonement for our sins and those of the whole world. For the sake of His Sorrowful Passion; Have mercy on us and on the whole world."

Soon I began falling, not into the peaceful slumber I had anticipated but through descending layers of darkness that left shadows dancing before my closed eyes. I could not control my thoughts in my dream, and with each breath, I felt a terrible fire burning in my lungs. Panic gripped me as I struggled to escape the noose that was being drawn tight around my neck. Having no arms to grasp the rope, I was left hanging midair. Kicking my legs, I fought an invisible phantom bent on my destruction while his minions encircled me, their leering green eyes taunting me with threats. I awoke to my own voice crying out, "Jesus!"

I tore frantically at the covers, now drenched in my sweat, and I rolled to my knees hitting the wooden floor with a thud. Arms violently shaking, I pushed myself up from the side of the bed and lunged toward the door. Flinging the door wide, I stumbled out onto the porch. Bent over gasping for air, I would never again delude myself that the battle had ended.

> "Be alert and of sober mind. Your enemy the devil prowls around like a roaring lion looking for someone to devour" (1 Pet. 5:8, NIV).

Covering the few steps to the hermitage where my sister slept, I knocked on her door. I related my terrifying dream to her as she slipped on her shoes. She pointed to the log chapel across the clearing and said, "Come on. Grab your shoes. Let's go."

We walked with purpose through the blanket of mist rising from the ground as I tried to shake the fog from my brain. The full moon had risen over the tall pines. Shining above the steeple of the chapel, it looked to me like a round unleavened wafer—a Host—suspended in space. We entered the chapel with only the moonlight streaming in through the windows to illuminate our way up the aisle. Kneeling before the altar, I gazed with relief at the light flickering from the Tabernacle lamp, its soft glow a reminder of the Lord's Eucharistic Presence. My heart slowly calmed as I knelt in the pew. I became giddy with joy knowing anything that the enemy brought against me would only drive me deeper into the Sacred Heart of Jesus, the very thing my heart desired. No longer afraid, I saw the truth that Satan poses no threat to Jesus and knowing I belonged to Him, I could not contain my happy laughter.

"The light shines in the darkness,
and the darkness has not overcome it"
(John 1:5, NIV).

The more time that passed after Ethan's bone marrow transplant, the more we began to think that the years of struggle with cancer were behind us. At seven years old, Ethan was finally cleared to attend kindergarten. However, he had barely been in school a month when a playground injury required a trip to the doctor. After an extensive round of tests were completed, we were called back to the children's hospital. There I listened in utter disbelief as I was informed that Ethan had developed a tumorous secondary cancer.

Once again, I sat in silent agony as his doctor explained the surgery that would take place and how it would affect Ethan's life, should he live. If Ethan survived, he'd never father children. *If* he survived. I rose, walked to the door and out of the room without a word, leaving Ethan's doctor staring after me. I found a deserted corridor and began to sing quietly.

> "I will bless the Lord at all times; His praise shall continually be in my mouth. My soul will glory in the Lord; let the humble hear and be glad. Oh, magnify the Lord with me, and let us exalt his name together! I sought the Lord, and he answered me and delivered me from all my fears (Ps. 34:1–4, NABRE).

I paced the empty hall. I began to praise God for all He was doing for Ethan. Even though it was not apparent from the report I had been given, I acknowledged that God would work it out for Ethan's good. I sang of God's promises for healing and deliverance from sickness and death. I thanked Him for His presence and His love. I reclaimed the ground that the enemy had stolen and demanded its return in Jesus's name. I blessed every cell of Ethan's body and blessed all those who were attempting to help us. I prayed, imploring God's angels to assist us and surround us with their protection and to keep us from harm.

"My flesh and my heart may fail, But
God is the rock and strength of my heart
and my portion forever" (Ps. 73:26, NIV).

I praised God's Holy Name, His power, His faithfulness, and recounted the wondrous deeds God had done for
His people throughout history. I recalled all He had done
for us in the past and reminded myself that He was and
is and always will be the same. I asked that Ethan's life be
spared. I declared that I believed God would make up to
Ethan all he suffered. I affirmed my belief that God could
replace all that was stolen from Ethan and would bless him
with supernatural wisdom and understanding of what was
happening.

I prayed the words that Jesus taught me to pray. The
words echoed in the vacant corridor as I sang, "Our Father
who art in heaven, hallowed be thy name; thy kingdom
come, thy will be done, on earth as it is in heaven. Give us
this day our daily bread and forgive us our trespasses, as we
forgive those who trespass against us, and lead us not into
temptation, but deliver us from evil." I prayed, "Not my
will Father, but Yours be done."

"In my distress, I called out: Lord! I
cried out to my God. From His Temple He
heard my voice. My cry to Him reached
His ears. He parted the heavens and came
down, a dark cloud under His feet. The
Lord thundered from heaven, the Most
High made His voice resound. He let fly

His arrows and scattered them, shot His lightning bolts and dispersed them. He reached down from on high and seized me. He set me free in the open: He rescued me because He loves me!" (Ps. 18:6, 9, 13, 14, 16, 19, NIV)

There in the hallway, fighting the feeling of impending doom, I closed my eyes and saw myself as a very small child sitting on the grass, engaged in play with a soft yellow kitten on my lap. The scene unfolded as I watched the kitten playfully scamper away. Toddling close behind the cat, I saw him climb inside the wheel well of my dad's enormous red dump truck in the driveway beside the house. Just as the engine roared, I reached out my small hand to stroke his silky coat. "Eileen!" I heard my name screamed, and turning my head, I was momentarily blinded by the sun. Then a brilliant flash of light and a face as gentle as it was fearsome eclipsed the sun in my eyes. I fell backward into the arms of, not my angelic apparition, but of my big sister.

Enfolded in a smothering hug, I was carried to the porch and safety. I cast a glance over my shoulder to see my father's truck pull away. Crying out, I wailed as I saw what was left of the kitten, crushed on the concrete. The scene ended abruptly. I swallowed hard as I recognized the opportunity I was being given. God was calling forth my woundedness to be healed, right there, right then in that hallway of the hospital.

The feeling I was presently having, of Ethan's impending doom, had triggered the memory and brought to mind the beliefs I had formed from my childhood experience; *that this would end badly* and *there was nothing I could do to stop it.* Those beliefs would prevent me from believing anything differently if I did not step out of agreement with those lies completely rejecting them as truth. As I opened my heart to correction and placed God's truth first in my mind, my perception of our predicament changed. My faith in God's plan was restored, and although I did not understand it, I would trust He would work it out for our good.

Finding my way back to the hospital meeting room, I opened the door and stepped into our next chapter. "We wondered if you were going to come back," Ethan's doctor said as he looked up from the treatment plan. He was sketching out the surgical procedure that would leave me without any doubt of the severity of this cancer. "I'm ready now," I calmly announced.

> *I abandon myself to you O Lord, my God, my Savior and my King, and to your mercy, to the intervention of the Most Holy Spirit, and to the intercession of Your Most Blessed Mother Mary, and to the prayers and the intentions of all your saints and angels in heaven, for the redemption of souls. Amen.*
> (Eileen's prayer)

We returned home long enough for Ethan to recover from the biopsy surgery, and I began calling friends to start another prayer chain throughout our church community.

Ethan was one of five little boys within a five-mile radius of our home who were all diagnosed with cancer. I received a call from one of the boy's mother. She had heard about Ethan's prognosis and wanted me to know that her prayer group members were praying for him. I shared my grief and she prayed with me, and then explained the real reason for her call, "Father George Fortuna will be here for my prayer cenacle tomorrow. I would like to ask him to come to your home to give Ethan his First Holy Communion. Please don't wait." I was torn between my feeling of joy that Ethan would receive a much needed, additional source of sacramental grace and the grief I felt as the reality struck. I would never see my son stand with a class of healthy seven-year-old children to make his First Communion.

When Father George arrived the next day, I led him into the bedroom where Ethan lay listless and pale against his pillow. I explained to Ethan why Father George had come. Sitting beside Ethan and holding his limp hand, Father George asked Ethan if he wanted to receive Jesus. When he nodded, he told Ethan that Jesus was present in Body, Blood, Soul, and Divinity in the consecrated Host he held in front of him. Ethan opened his mouth to receive the Blessed Eucharist, then at once, closed his eyes. Father then anointed him with the oil of the sacrament of the sick, leaving us with a blessing for comfort, peace, and courage.

When the appointed day for Ethan's surgery arrived, I took heart knowing Jesus had come to strengthen Ethan in a very real way for what was about to happen. I donned a scrub suit in the waiting room and lifted Ethan into my arms carrying him down the hall toward the operating room as I had so many times before. I told the unfamiliar nurse who stepped forward and tried to bar my way that this is how it was going to be done. She glanced at the attendant who shrugged, her arms weighted down carrying my son's medical files, nearly two feet thick. Moving out of the way, the nurse conceded, "All right, I can see you have been here before."

Upon entering the operating room, we personally greeted everyone there. We went through our routine of thanking them for being there to take care of Ethan and explained that we would be praying for them while they were working to help him feel better. Ethan explained to them how he would like to fall asleep in my arms—with medicine, not the mask. I assured Ethan I would stay close and he would see me when he woke up. As I left the room, I blessed each of them, proclaimed aloud a blessing on the room, asking God's angels to remain there to assist the staff.

Many times, speaking out in faith does not come naturally. It feels awkward. It tests your beliefs and your convictions. As soon as the words pass your lips, the doubt begins to percolate, and it takes a strong will to pull the plug. If, after standing in faith, someone confronts you with doubt, it is a dangerous temptation to succumb to the urge to plunge headlong into fear and despair all over again.

Viktor Frankl, Austrian neurologist, psychiatrist, and Holocaust survivor, knew about this "space of faith." He wrote in *Man's Search for Meaning*, "Between stimulus and response, there is a space. In that space is our power to choose our response." It is a space to think and to pray. It is our opportunity to recall what we have already chosen and by habit choose again.

The day after surgery, Ethan and I were shown to a room where we awaited Ethan's doctor, who had overseen his case from the beginning of his treatment. I knew the news was not good when Ethan's doctor came in and informed me that he would no longer be seeing us, that he was handing Ethan's case over to another doctor. "I'm sorry, there is nothing more that we can do. This change means I can no longer be his doctor. We can only give Ethan more chemotherapy to buy you some more time to make peace with this, but there is nothing more that can be done to help him."

It had been a very brutal four-year battle. I stared at Ethan who lay curled up on my lap wrapped in his baby blanket waiting to go home—always waiting to go home. I felt the icy grip of a new anguish clutch my heart as I pulled my son close, wishing God would whisk us both away. I imagined us back in the magical birds' nest of pillows and comforters on our living room floor with our girls. Trying hard to swallow the growing lump in my throat that was threatening to cut off my breath, I reached out and took the treatment schedule from Ethan's doctor's hand and nodded my understanding. "Can we go home now?" Ethan begged. "Yes. We are leaving," I assured him, the words *just for the night* silently echoing in my aching heart.

That night after tucking him into bed and softly singing him to sleep, I walked to my room and quietly closed the door. Dropping to the floor at the foot of my bed, I closed my eyes and began to petition God's throne, begging for His glory to be shown. For hours, I tossed between torment over what I was to do and trust, knowing my circumstance did not change who God was. He was and forever would be faithful, forever trustworthy, forever holy, and good. I cried out of my heart, "You are merciful! You *alone* are the Lord! You *alone* are the Mighty One! You are God Almighty, and worthy of all my praise! Yours is the power. Yours is the glory! I love you, Lord God, and I exalt Your Holy Name no matter what is happening!"

Grace was falling, and I lifted both arms to catch it. With upturned hands, I reached for my God. "Father, I need you. I know You have a plan for us although I cannot see it. You are with us in our time of trouble! You are compassionate. You have not forsaken us! You are our Vindicator and Healer. I know You hear my prayer! You are the Rock beneath my feet. Shine Your light to show me the way! You make up for what I lack. Jesus, I trust You. Jesus, I trust You!" I cried.

Finally resting in God's comfort, I paused in my prayer. I felt my spirit shore up my soul, words forming and passing through my mind. "Let nothing trouble you, let nothing make you afraid. All things pass away. Patience obtains everything. God alone is enough. In your struggles is proof of your love and the more you will rejoice one day with your Beloved in happiness and peace that will never end. Hope, soul! Hope! You know neither the day nor the hour of His coming. Watch carefully, for everything passes quickly even though your impatience makes doubtful what is certain and turns a very short time into a much longer one."

"For He will command His angels concerning you to guard you in all of your ways" (Ps. 91:11, NIV).

The voice I sensed was not a stranger. Long ago, answering my prayer to God for help, the voice had revealed its presence and purpose to me. I allowed my guardian angel *James* to fight the battle of fear and despair as I rested in God's Divine Will. I knew that *James* (his name meaning to supplant the enemy by force and strategy) neither left my side nor failed to behold the face of God. I was assured that Ethan's angel as well would guard him through our most terrible night.

"See that you do not despise one of these little ones. For I tell you that in heaven their angels always see the face of my Father who is in heaven" (Matt. 18:10, NIV).

Early the next morning, we went through the same routine that we had gone through repeatedly for over three years. I woke Ethan slowly. After finding the softest clothing he had, I warmed them in the dryer. I dressed him and then while singing silly songs to distract him I loaded him into the car. Inseparable from his baby blankets, I tucked them securely around Ethan as I buckled him into his car seat, leaving a portion folded against his cheek to cushion his head. We began plotting the fun things we would do later in the day, his weak and strained voice repeating each idea after me. However, today would not end the same and one decision would change the course of our life forever.

As the children's hospital came into view, Ethan began to weep softly. The sound of his woeful cry caused me to grip the steering wheel tightly. I drew a steadying breath in, silently praying one word, "Jesus!" as I exhaled. In my mind I saw the frightened and confused three-year-old I had brought to this place years ago, who trusted me to somehow protect him from every terrifying procedure and protocol that we obediently followed. The vision moved to the four-year-old who had been coerced into enduring painful treatments and tests, as we routinely dealt with the cycles of weakness and misery, while the whole time covertly designing plans and tricks to make our escape. I then saw the five-year-old who angrily and indignantly fought for his life through a bone morrow transplant, defiantly and emphatically proclaiming he was not sick. Now weak and despairing, this six-year-old mournfully whimpered, pathetically crying, "Mommy, *please*! Please don't make me go back in there . . . I hate the tools they use to hurt children!" Upon hearing his words, my heart was indescribably pierced, and I audibly gasped as everything suddenly became crystal-clear. I felt as if blinders I had been wearing were suddenly ripped from my eyes. I had a choice. In that instant, the choice was made. "We are going in there, Ethan, but only to tell them we are not coming back."

As the nurse approached to "welcome" us to the pediatric infusion room, I squared my shoulders and silently planted my feet in the Lord's Camp as I had so many times before. I did not think at the time that I had "heard" any directive from God. It felt like common sense finally reigned in me with enough strength to voice the truth in my heart. I now understood my position and could insist that the protocol they were offering was not absolute. I would finally be taking Ethan for what we would forevermore call a "second opinion."

> "Therefore put on the full armor of God, so that when the day of evil comes, you may be able to stand your ground, and after you have done everything, to stand. Stand firm then, with the belt of truth buckled around your waist, with the breastplate of righteousness in place, and with your feet fitted with the readiness that comes from the gospel of peace. In addition to all this, take up the shield of faith, with which you can extinguish all the flaming arrows of the evil one. Take the helmet of salvation and the sword of the Spirit, which is the word of God." (Eph. 6:13–17, NIV)

CHAPTER 7
Kindness

"So we can say with confidence, 'The
Lord is my helper, so I will have no fear.
What can mere people do to me?'"
—Hebrews 13:6 (NIV)

Once back home, I began a wild scramble to contact every-one I knew who had cancer, or anyone who knew someone who had any experience with cancer and who did anything outside of the conventional medical or pharmaceutical treatment. The phone rang for days as doctors, nurses, social workers, and administrators from the children's hospital repeatedly called insisting that Ethan needed to con-tinue treatment and insinuating neglect if I did not bring him back into the hospital. I explained to the first two who called that I understood the prognosis and they would hear from me after getting our second opinion. Further calls I erased from my message machine unheard. I turned all my energy to following the Holy Spirit as I prayed for direc-tion. I followed leads until a door opened or closed.

"In God I have put my trust, I shall
not be afraid. What can man do to me?"
(Ps. 56:11, NASB).

I remembered that a friend, the mother of one of the children in treatment, had mentioned she was doing some "natural" treatments with her son. I dialed the phone, and when she answered, I confided, "There is nothing more they can do for Ethan." She listened to the diagnosis then told me she had taken her son to see Doug Leber, a holistically trained doctor in Texas. She highly recommended I do the same. I had heard the term *holistic* before from our chiropractor and knew that he understood the body in ways that a medical doctor was not trained.

Thankfully, Ethan and I would not travel alone to Texas. My friend's husband was taking their son to an appointment and we were able to arrange a flight and appointment at the same time. I was terrified of taking Ethan on a plane in fear of infection, after avoiding public places for so long. However, God had again provided for us with a seasoned guide to help us with this new experience. On the long flight, I listened as my friend's husband calmed and encouraged his son. At the same time, I felt God calming and encouraging us.

I called Doug Leber's office once we landed in Texas and had settled in at the motel. I was told by the staff to wait in our motel room and call the office back every two hours to see what the status was on the doctor's schedule. They would then estimate when we should head over to the office from the motel. Once they outlined the unfamiliar system to me, I began to pray to control the hysteria as all my misgivings began to parade through my mind. Our appointment was at 11:00 a.m. in the morning. At 4:00 p.m., we were finally told to head over to Dr. Leber's office to wait at the clinic.

I had been told that Doug Leber was called the Sherlock Holmes of electrodermal screening. Once he was on the trail of his patient's disease, he would tenaciously follow it until he discovered the culprit—the root cause. Baffled at first by their scheduling system, I would later bless Doug Leber when it was Ethan's mystery he was unraveling.

Sitting in the waiting room, I cradled Ethan's hairless head, as he lay limp against my shoulder. I closed my eyes hoping to keep back the tears of distress and exhaustion that threatened to spill. Gently I kissed Ethan's head. Praying for strength, I finally opened my eyes to see a distinguished gentleman with deep and gentle eyes standing before me. Dr. Lee Cowden introduced himself as the medical doctor on staff. He spoke softly and confidently, "Don't worry, Mother, God led you here. You are in the right place." As he turned and left the room, I felt the air I had been holding in my lungs escape and peace fill me once again.

My first impression of Dr. Leber was that of a humble scholar. No white coat was worn to shroud arrogance or pride, and he preferred we call him Doug. He showed me to a seat and briefly explained I would hold Ethan on my lap and offer his hand or foot to be prodded by a stylus that was attached to the computer. We watched as he touched each of Ethan's acupressure points and an image was transferred to his computer screen. I endeavored to distract Ethan and keep him still.

Engrossed in his work, Dr. Doug Leber completely ignored us and seemed undisturbed by Ethan's restless complaints and tired cries. He rose and left the room only once in four hours to return with a glass of water and continue his probing.

When he finally finished, Doug turned to me with a pleased smile and said, "Ethan has benzene in his bone marrow." My dazed look prompted him to add, "Benzene is a petroleum byproduct that is known to cause childhood leukemia. We can help his body to remove it." I was speechless. "There are many additional issues that need to be resolved, including heavy metals, parasites and viruses that need to be removed." My shock turned quickly into burning anger. Absolutely no one in four years at the children's hospital had ever had a conversation with me about toxicity having anything to do with Ethan's illness. Why had the importance of eliminating toxins never been addressed?

Drawing on the habitual practice of taking every ounce of pleasure that we could out of *any* good news we received, I quickly shook off the talons of bitterness that I was feeling. It was as if I had been given a map to escape after years of being trapped in a maze. My mind careened frantically as it raced to connect all the broken dots. Doug continued to use his probe to find the most effective remedies from a list of natural substances programmed into his computer. I was preoccupied with my thoughts and was remembering that after Ethan's initial diagnosis I had prayed with a man from The Franciscan University in Steubenville, who had come to speak at a Divine Mercy Conference I attended. Praying over Ethan, he had told me that he sensed the Lord revealing that the cause of Ethan's illness was environmental. At the time it did not even register to me what that could have meant. Now it was becoming clear.

As Doug briefly explained the reasons for the degeneration in Ethan's body, I began to see how his disease came to be. Ethan had been prescribed round after round of antibiotics since birth, having had several eye surgeries, asthma, and catching every illness that went around in my day care. I had no idea of the damage caused by overuse of those routinely prescribed antibiotics, or as Doug explained, how imperative it was to replace and recolonize the body's good bacteria when they were destroyed from the medication.

I had certainly not understood the repercussions to Ethan's liver when it was recommended I use acetaminophen to relieve his pain and fever, or how damaging it was in combination with vaccinations he was given. It never occurred to me to be concerned about parasites that can be ingested when drinking unfiltered water, eating out or handling pets. I now understood how they could seriously wreak havoc and complicate the body's ability to heal. As the stronghold of blissful ignorance began to crumble, it was replaced in my mind by an image of scattered pieces of a brain-teaser-puzzle or Rubik's cube, the pieces now all sliding together to form a solid square.

As Doug explained the common household toxins that contained benzene, I pictured the mounds of plastic toys in my day care and the strong smells they emitted. It also brought to mind the harsh chemical sanitation process we used to clean the toys at the end of each day. I connected it to new carpet and new car smell. I felt ill knowing I had benzene paints, glues, and other caustic chemical cleaners at home. Since I had no garage, they were stored in my hallway utility closet. I also recalled my dad's death from cancer and all the harsh chemicals he had worked with as a builder. I fought tears remembering my brother Nicky and the last glimpse I had of him as he lay dying of cancer in the army hospital in Texas. Hadn't I heard he was exposed to Agent Orange in Vietnam?

When I read the long list of toxins that were present in Ethan's body and the deficient vitamins and minerals that were listed on the computer screen in front of me, my heart sank. When Doug explained the source of the toxins and how depleted his body had become, my stomach turned. Immediately, I recounted the short distance between the children's chemo infusion room and the fast-food restaurant in the hospital. I thought of the irony of how the hospital had served chemical chemotherapy cocktails and cancer-causing food ingredients to the same patients. I also thought of the state funded food program we were encouraged to use in the day care that endorsed processed boxed and canned products with a prolonged shelf life. I now realized it was at the expense of providing any living nourishment to the children in my care.

I was shocked at the amount of lead, aluminum, mercury, and other heavy metals in Ethan's body. Questioning Doug on how that had happened, he explained that there were many sources, even in drinking water as well as vaccinations and the chemotherapy my son had been given. My thoughts drifted back to when I was eighteen years old and to the first time I had read over the fact sheet given to me when I took my firstborn to be vaccinated. I now wondered how it had made any sense to me to put the substances of those vaccines into my child's body. I remember the trepidation I ignored when I read over the possible side effects that could result from the injection, *including death*, listed clearly on the consent form they handed me. It upset me so badly that day that I decided never to read those forms again. As if that could protect us! Was that the reaction of frightened young mothers everywhere? Did we all indiscriminately trust the doctors' recommendations without questioning whether the ingredients in the shots were something we wanted in our child's body? How was I completely blind to the dangers printed in black and white right in front of me? Had I even been told whether or not there was a single, double blind, placebo-controlled study assessing the long-term risks of childhood vaccinations?

I took a deep breath to stop the guilt and dread that was rising in me. I realized that so many of the toxins listed on Ethan's test were there because of things that I had never questioned or was totally unaware would affect him. Sensing my panic, Doug explained to me that as the toxins were removed with help from the remedies, and with the necessary organ support, Ethan's body could heal. I left Doug's office after 10:00 p.m. that night knowing the cause of Ethan's cancer and holding a list of remedies to remove it gripped tightly in my hand.

Returning home much more optimistic than when we had left, I felt I was walking on air when I finally tucked Ethan into his own bed. Taking advantage of the time I had while Ethan was asleep, I sat at the kitchen counter meticulously labeling dozens of bottles of homeopathic tinctures and herbs, lining them up like soldiers ready for battle. I organized them into groups charting the time of day, dosage and marking those taken with or between meals. I placed the small day-care television and video player in the bathroom where I would need to keep Ethan in the bathtub for a forty-five-minute detox bath two to three times a day.

I fought to hold back my tears, overcome this time with hope instead of despair, yet unnerved by the gravity of what I was doing. As I looked down at the remedies, I realized I was taking responsibility for changing Ethan's prognosis and I began to tremble. Fears began to fill my mind. "What if this doesn't work? What if there isn't time for it to work? What if I can't get these remedies into him? What if it makes him worse?"

Suddenly, the thought dawned on me. "What was worse than death? What could be worse than already being told there was no hope?" I firmly planted my feet in the Lord's camp *again* and resolved to fight those fears with trust that God was leading me, and His grace would keep me, whatever happened. I had given the children's hospital years of our lives, convinced the benefits would somehow outweigh the risk. That, however, turned out not to be the case, and I had been told that all known treatment there was exhausted.

When Ethan was first diagnosed, I was quoted percentages and five-year survival rates for children with his type of cancer. Had they really meant five years of life was all we were to expect? Had they meant that five years was how long it took for children taking chemotherapy to die? Had I been completely charmed by their presentation of a treatment, *any treatment*, that I became blind when I read that cancer was a possible side effect of the chemotherapy? Was there a reason that I was *not told* there was more that I personally could do to increase the chance of my child surviving?

My thoughts were excruciatingly painful. By default, thoughts are negative being nature's way of motivating us to think the worst will happen, so we will take shelter in an approaching storm or run from a tiger. The opportunity for preventing Ethan's health disaster had passed. We were in the midst of it and I needed to stay in the present moment. I needed to stay tuned in to the Holy Spirit's prompting and move forward without fear, never doubting that He was leading me. The journey was worth the lessons I would learn along the way. I needed to learn to trust that God would continue to deposit His grace as needed.

> "We demolish arguments and every pretension that sets itself up against the knowledge of God, and we take captive every thought to make it obedient to Christ" (2 Cor. 10:5, NIV).

When each doubt arose, I replaced my own thoughts with God's thoughts. I dug through the Scriptures daily searching for direction. Systematically, routinely, purposely, and patiently, I prayed. I encouraged myself that with God's help we would find the way. I clung to the truth of His promises and would not let go.

I changed my focus from both what was in the past and what lie in the future, onto what was right in front of me. It was more important to know who God was than to understand what He was doing. It was more crucial to spend time with Him than to spend time trying to make something happen. It was more essential for me to contemplate His immeasurable love than to endeavor to somehow earn His love and approval. Secure in nothing but God's love for us, I moved in the direction He was leading me.

JESUS

You are the One, the Father's
Son; come among the ones
Who call the Father through
the Son, who love the Father
through His only Son.
Jesus
You are the Two, the Father
lives in You; in all you do
The Father's love is known through You.
The Father's love is known
through all you do.
Jesus
You are the Three, you sent
the Paraclete; to set us free
Through the mystery of the Holy Trinity,
through the love between you and me.
Jesus
(Song by Eileen)

Once I made the connection between the petroleum toxin benzene and my son's leukemia, there was no going back. Relentless, I began removing the toxins that were under my control from Ethan's environment. It was well before the easy access of a Google search, so I read and reread books written by the experts on toxins and cancer. I poured over the chapters on parasites, benzene, and heavy metals, all which were found in my son's body and contributed to his illness. I followed the advice to purge our household of every possible carcinogenic suspect.

Within hours of returning home from Texas, we had a dozen garbage bags of personal body products, cleaning products, toys, paraffin candles, and processed foods from every corner and cupboard thrown out in the trash. I was again amazed and blessed as my teenage girls willingly pitched their fragrances, sprays, nail polish, and polish removers. Anything that posed a threat to Ethan's recovery went in the bags.

Electro-magnetic fields that we learned would hinder Ethan's cellular repair caused me to turn off our electricity at night. I understood it would be important to have a period of time when Ethan's body could heal without the stress of free radicals created by electronics or electricity. We turned off the main electrical breaker for the whole house for ten hours each night. This meant we would be possessed to drag our refrigerator, the only thing that absolutely needed power, out onto the deck to be connected by extension cord to the outdoor garage outlet.

Growing accustomed to stumbling around the house at night with a flashlight, we eventually fell into a routine. I thanked God for my daughters' willingness to sacrifice their comfort for Ethan's sake. I watched my girls wrapped in their robes, hair in towel, stepping outside to grab a snack, poking their head under the tarp that was protecting the refrigerator from the elements. Though inconvenient, more times than not, it was a source of comic relief as we marveled at the absurdity of it all. A new respect grew for the people in homes we sometimes passed who had makeshift apparatuses and appliances on their porch or in their front yard. Desperate people are drawn to desperate measures.

I struggled to maintain some semblance of normalcy for our family as we attempted to bring balance into our changing world once again. However, this time we had purpose and hope. We were doing something meaningful that would have an impact on the quality of all our lives. Filled with the vision of what making these changes could mean for Ethan's recovery, we began learning what alternatives to use as we cleaned up our personal environmental toxins. I was increasing my family's nutrition at every single meal with simple organic whole foods and it felt good. It felt right. We agreed we were all in this together. It took all of us to support one another when one of us became weak and tempted to give in or give up.

I could no longer ignore the fact that I still needed to find continued medical care for Ethan. The organization that was helping with unpaid medical and transportation costs had a change in policy and notified me they could only financially assist further treatments if they were performed in a medical hospital. I needed to find a medical doctor to oversee his progress and keep close watch for infection, the spread of cancer and to monitor his blood counts. I needed someone who understood what we had learned about how the body healed and who would stay true to the Hippocratic Oath to "first do no harm." I followed leads until I could go no further. I prayed, then listened, to know when to change course and when to stand and wait.

I discovered many health clinics were helping people to recover from cancer but were now no longer accessible to me or anyone else who did not have the financial resources. There were health professionals excelling in natural medicine that included MDs, DOs, and naturopaths, working with herbalists, acupuncturists, colon therapists, and massage therapists. There were whole food nutritionists and practitioners schooled in Chinese medicine and homeopathy. Yet all beyond my reach because medical insurance would not cover the methods and I could not personally provide the cost. Feeling the familiar panic begin to press in on me from all sides, I dedicated myself to another nine-day novena asking for the powerful intercession of Saint Joseph, spouse and protector of the Virgin Mary (Matt. 1:18–24).

> "In the same way, the Spirit helps us in our weakness. We do not know what we ought to pray for, but the Spirit himself intercedes for us with groans that words cannot express. And he who searches our hearts knows the mind of the Spirit, because the Spirit intercedes for the saints in accordance with God's will." (Rom. 8:26–27, NIV)

Word then came to me from a friend of a friend about a hospital in Mexico that was known for its natural healing practices. I immediately contacted the Oasis of Hope Hospital in Tijuana, Mexico (http://www.oasisofhope. com). After speaking with the receptionist, I was told Dr. Francisco Contreras would be calling me personally for a consultation, and our new plan began to take shape. All that I needed now was for Ethan's pediatrician to write a letter acceptable to the board of the organization that had agreed to financially assist us.

> "Be strong and bold; have no fear or
> dread of them, because it is the Lord your
> God who goes with you; he will not fail
> you or forsake you" (Deut. 31:6, NRSV).

Ethan had been diagnosed with leukemia in 1997, and here I was standing in that same room nearly four years later waiting for my son's pediatrician. I greatly respected and fondly loved our pediatrician. My older sisters' children were among his very first patients when he opened his practice. Among us, our family had remained his patients for over thirty years.

All through Ethan's medical treatment, I heeded every word my pediatrician spoke, valuing his compassionate care, believing Ethan's life depended on it. I had blindly followed his directives—metaphorically clinging to his white coat tails—and the authority they represented. Nevertheless, I was not the same naïve mother that had tearfully accepted a cookie-cutter assembly line resolution to what I discovered was a very personalized and complex disease.

Now I stood with my eyes wide open. I nervously waited for his response to my request for the letter I needed. I had no illusions. My child and his recovery were my responsibility. There would not be anyone in white coats standing beside me mourning at my son's graveside if he did not recover.

I was following a greater authority. My heart was leading me and the conviction in my spirit was giving me courage to stand my ground. The doctor entered the room and squarely faced me. He insisted I had the best of care at the children's hospital and would not receive that kind of care in Mexico. He had seen that kind of "natural medicine" in India, and it was exactly why he came to the United States to practice real medicine. He cautioned me not to throw away money by chasing after an unproven cure.

I stared in disbelief. How could I not? His Western medicine gave us no more hope! I did not want quality care while I watched my son die. I wanted to be where they would help me fight for his life without further destroying his body! I could feel the fire in my heart course through my veins with every objection he presented until my face burned. I realized it would only be by the grace of God that I would leave with his consent letter for the board.

> "For I am the LORD your God who takes hold of your right hand and says to you, 'Do not fear; I will help you'" (Isa. 41:13, NIV).

Already my mind was struggling to devise another way to achieve my goal. Restraining myself, I silently breathed, "Jesus, I trust you." Abruptly, the pediatrician turned and left the room. Returning shortly, he handed me his office letterhead with the hastily written declaration, "I understand that Eileen will be taking her son to the Oasis of Hope Hospital in Tijuana, Mexico, for further evaluation and treatment." He then said, "I know you feel you must do this. I don't agree, but I understand." My eyes filled with tears of gratitude for what he was able to do, and I prayed the board would accept the pediatrician's letter as consent.

> "Whenever the cloud was lifted from over the tent, afterward the sons of Israel would then set out; and in the place where the cloud settled down, there the sons of Israel would camp. At the command of the LORD the sons of Israel would set out, and at the command of the LORD they would camp; as long as the cloud settled over the tabernacle, they remained camped." (Num. 9:17–18, NASB)

Late that night when the house became quiet, I sat staring down at the stack of treatment "fact sheets" that I had been given since Ethan was first diagnosed with cancer. Knowing now that the cause of the leukemia was a toxic level of benzene in his body, I read through the list of all my son had suffered from his treatment, with new enlightened eyes:

THE CANCER TREATMENTS OF AMERICA WEB SITE: SIDE EFFECTS

Methotrexate (Mexate):
- Headache
- Dizziness
- Drowsiness
- Swollen, tender gums
- Decreased appetite
- Reddened eyes
- Hair loss
- Mouth sores
- Diarrhea
- Black, tarry, or blood stools
- Vomit that is bloody
- Fever, sore throat, cough, chills,
- Blisters or peeling skin
- Blurred vision or loss of vision
- Seizures
- Confusion
- Weakness or difficulty moving
- Loss of consciousness

Cyclophosphamide (Cytoxan)
- Nausea
- Vomiting
- Loss of appetite
- Abdominal pain
- Diarrhea

- Weight loss
- Mouth or tongue sores
- Changes in skin color
- Changes in fingernails/toenails
- Sore throat, fever, chills,
- Signs of infection
- Poor or slow wound healing
- Unusual bruising or bleeding
- Black, tarry stools
- Painful urination
- Hives, rash, itching
- Difficulty breathing/ swallowing
- Shortness of breath
- Swelling in the legs, ankles, feet
- Chest pain
- Yellowing of the skin or eyes

Prednisone (oral)
- Increased appetite
- Irritability
- Difficulty sleeping (insomnia)
- Swelling in your ankles and feet

- Nausea, take with food
- Heartburn
- Muscle weakness
- Impaired wound healing
- Increased blood sugar levels
- Headaches
- Dizziness
- Mood swings
- Cataracts and bone thinning

Vincristine (injection)
- Blurred or double vision
- Constipation
- Difficulty in waiting
- Drooping eyelids
- Headache
- Jaw pain
- Joint pain
- Lower back or side pain
- Numbness/tingling fingers/ toes
- Pain in fingers and toes
- Pain in testicles
- Stomach cramps
- Swelling of feet or lower legs
- Weakness

- Agitation
- Bed-wetting
- Confusion
- Convulsions (seizures)
- Decrease or increase in urination
- Dizziness or lightheadedness
- Hallucinations
- Lack of sweating
- Loss of appetite
- Mental depression
- Painful or difficult urination
- Trouble in sleeping
- Unconsciousness
- Sores in mouth and on lips
- Neuritic pain
- Loss of deep-tendon reflexes,
- Foot drop
- Wrist drop
- Slapping gait
- Ataxia
- Paralysis
- Cranial nerve manifestations
- Isolated paresis
- Paralysis of muscles
- Jaw pain
- Pharyngeal pain
- Parotid gland pain
- Bone pain, back pain
- Limb pain
- Myalgia

- Pain may be severe
- Convulsions
- Hypertension
- Acute fulminant encephalopathy
- Severe mental confusion
- Coma

6-Thioguanine

- Nausea
- Vomiting
- Loss of appetite or weight
- Sores in the mouth and throat
- Headache
- Unusual tiredness or weakness
- Unusual bleeding or bruising
- Yellowing of the skin or eyes
- Flu-like symptoms
- Swelling of the stomach area
- Stomach pain, particularly in the right part of the stomach
- Swelling of the face, arms, hands, feet, ankles or lower legs
- Bloody vomit
- Black, tarry or bloody stools
- Fever, sore throat, ongoing cough

congestion, signs of infection
- Shortness of breath
- Lightheadedness

Adriamycin

- Nausea and vomiting that may last twenty-four to forty-eight hours after treatment
- Loss of appetite
- Diarrhea
- Difficulty swallowing
- Thinned or brittle hair
- An increased risk infection
- Hard to fight infections/very ill
- Headaches
- Aching muscles
- Cough
- Sore throat
- Pain passing urine
- Cold and shivery
- Anemia
- need a blood transfusion
- Bruising Nosebleeds
- Bleeding gums
- Tiny red spots/ bruises/petechial
- Feeling or being sick
- Diarrhea, abdominal pain

- A sore mouth
- or mouth ulcers
- Loss of appetite
- Sickness
- Diarrhea
- Sore mouth
- Loss of fertility
- Red eyes sensitive to light
- Watery eyes
- Red and inflamed skin
- Hair loss
- High uric acid levels
- Soreness at the injection site
- Aching muscles and bones
- Inflammation of heart
- Headaches
- Lung infections/ breathlessness
- A sore throat
- Liver changes
- Dizziness
- Difficulty passing urine
- Blood clots
- Kidney changes

Co-Trimoxazole,
Trimethoprim-Sulfa
(Bactrim, Seprta)
- Abdominal or stomach pain
- Black, tarry stools

- Blistering, peeling, loose skin
- Changes in skin color
- Chest pain
- Chills
- Skin irritation/rash on areas previously exposed to radiation treatments
- Darkening fingernails/ toenails
- Swelling, pain, redness, or peeling of skin on palms and soles of feet
- Fatigue
- Mouth blistering
- Unusual bleeding or bruising
- Red urine or sweat
- Pain where the drug was injected
- Cough or hoarseness
- Dark urine
- Diarrhea
- Dizziness
- Fever with or without chills
- General feeling of tiredness
- Weakness
- Headache
- Itching
- Joint or muscle pain
- Light-colored stools

- Loss of appetite
- Lower back or side pain
- Nausea
- Pain, tender, swelling foot/ leg
- Painful or difficult urination
- Pale skin
- Rash
- Red skin lesions
- Red, irritated eyes
- Shortness of breath
- Sore throat
- Sores, ulcers, mouth or lips
- Swollen or painful glands
- Tightness in the chest
- Unpleasant breath odor
- Unusual bleeding or bruising
- Vomiting of blood
- Wheezing
- Yellow eyes or skin
- Abdominal/ stomach tenderness
- Tender back, leg, stomach pains
- Bleeding gums
- Blindness or vision changes
- Blisters, hives, or itching
- Bloating
- Blood in the urine or stools

- Bluish lips/fingernails/palms
- Burning, crawling, itching
- Numbness, pain, tingling feelings
- Burning of the face or mouth
- Chest pain
- Cloudy urine
- Confusion
- Constipation
- Ringing/ buzzing/ noise in ears
- Convulsions
- Cracks in the skin
- Persistent diarrhea or other bowel changes
- Sore throat, fever, chills or other signs of infection
- Breathing discomfort

Cytarabine (Ara-C)
- Tiredness and breathlessness
- Drop in the number blood cell
- Decrease amount of urine
- Decrease frequency of urine
- Diarrhea, watery, severe, stool
- Bloody stools
- Difficulty with breathing

- Difficulty with swallowing
- Fainting spells
- General body swelling
- Discomfort or illness
- Hair loss
- Hearing loss
- Hives
- Increased thirst
- Indigestion
- Irregular heartbeat
- Large, purple patches in the skin
- Large, hive-like swelling of face
- Swollen eyelids, lips, tongue
- Swelling of throat, hands, legs
- Swollen feet, or sex organs
- Loss of heat from the body
- Muscle or joint pain
- Nosebleeds
- Not able to pass urine
- Numb/tingling hands, feet, lips
- Pain or burning while urinating
- Pinpoint red spots on the skin
- Puffiness eyes
- Swollen face, lips, or tongue

- Welts on skin/buttocks/legs/
- Swollen ankles
- Redness of whites of eyes
- Redness/swelling/sore tongue
- Sores/white spots mouth
- Sores on lips or in the mouth
- Soreness of the muscles
- Stiff neck or back
- Swelling of face/hands/legs/feet
- Unsteadiness, trembling
- Problems with muscle control
- Problem with coordination
- Unusual weight loss
- Weakness in the hands or feet
- Weakness/heaviness of the legs
- Weight gain
- Passing of gas
- Discouragement
- Feeling of constant movement
- Movement of self/surroundings
- Feeling sad or empty
- Sensitivity of skin to sunlight

- Irritability
- Lack of feeling or emotion
- Loss of interest or pleasure
- Nervousness
- Redness / discoloration of skin
- Seeing/hearing/feeling things
- Seeing things that are not there
- Sensation of spinning
- Severe sunburn
- Trouble concentrating
- Trouble sleeping

- Uncaring
- Weight loss

Radiation (total body, brain and testicular)
- Weight loss
- Radiation damage to heart/lungs
- Thyroid Problems
- Problem w/ hormone-making glands
- Problems with fertility
- Damage to bones
- Problems with bone growth

Development of another cancer (including leukemia) years later
- Bone Marrow Transplant Infections.
- Low platelets and low red blood cells
- Pain Fluid overload
- Respiratory distress
- Organ damage
- Graft failure
- Graft-versus-host disease

How could the level of benzene in my son's bone marrow ever be reduced by what they had administered? Why was the cause not even addressed? How had I been convinced to agree to these treatments again and again, year after year? As I read through the list, I could not stop the tears streaming from my eyes as I realized there was very little listed that Ethan did not painfully suffer. Those "side effects" had controlled and diminished his quality of life as well as all of us who loved and lived with him. I considered the side effects of treating him holistically with natural remedies. I was told the worst "side effects" would be a flu-like healing response. Again, I could see where I once was blind. I felt a sense of peace and reminded myself that God counted every tear we had cried; they had not gone unheeded.

"You keep track of all my sorrows. You
have collected all my tears in your bottle.
You have recorded each one in your book"
(Ps. 56:8, NLT).

Our tickets were arranged. The Oasis of Hope Hospital
in Tijuana, Mexico, was our destination. We were all committed to our new direction. It was a tear-filled goodbye as
I left my eighteen-year-old daughter Rochelle to care for
my ten-year-old daughter Claire. Leah, Ethan's bone morrow donor, would come with me to help with Ethan.

I remained relatively calm until we landed in San
Diego to meet the bus that would take us across the border to Oasis of Hope Hospital. I was encouraged when the
woman at the desk assured me that someone would come
soon to pick us up. I watched the minutes' tick their way
around the clock overhead as people rushed passed by to
catch their flights. For Ethan and Leah's sake, I silenced
each what-if that came to my mind and behind a cheerful façade tried to give the impression that we were on an
adventurous vacation instead of a harrowing attempt to
save Ethan's life.

Within the hour, we were loaded into a road van and
instructed what to do and say in preparation for crossing
the border. My heart pounding in my chest as our van
approached the border gate, my hand trembling as I tightly
clutched our passports and medical clearance. I could feel
the silent judgment of those back home, who were opposed
to our coming, tearfully predicting it would not end well.

The armed guards slowly approached both sides of our vehicle. Instinctively, I pulled Ethan closer and fervently prayed that Our Lady of Guadalupe, patroness of Mexico, would cover us in her mantle of love and protection. My racing thoughts began to subside when it then occurred to me that this must be routine to our driver. We weren't the first nor, God willing, the last to make this trip from the United States to the hospital in Mexico. Glancing briefly inside at us, the guards conversed in Spanish then signaled the driver to move ahead. As we passed through the gate, I breathed, "Thank You, Jesus!" and smiled at Leah, beginning to relax my firm hold on Ethan's frail body.

I was relieved to see a large though modest, salmon-colored hospital as we passed the marquee announcing our arrival at the Oasis of Hope Hospital. Gathering our belongings, we walked across the warm terra cotta floor to the reception area. The woman at the registration desk welcomed us softly in English, assuring us that everything was being taken care of and handing me the necessary papers encouraged us not to worry about a thing.

Once inside the elevator on our way to our assigned room, I closed my eyes to keep the tears from escaping. A world away from family and support I wearily leaned against the wall. I opened my eyes to a Scripture verse framed on the wall in front of me. "The Lord, your God, is in your midst, a Mighty Savior. He will take great delight in you, He will quiet you with his love, He will rejoice over you with singing" (Zep. 3:17, NIV). Slowly and deeply, I began to breathe again.

We were soon settled into our room where we would spend most of our time for the next three and a half weeks. I stared at the sign above the bathroom sink that warned us not to swallow any water while showering and cautioned us not to accidentally drink it while brushing our teeth. I had been conditioned for four long years to control our environment for fear of infection and the irony caused me to shake my head at what I had gotten us into.

While Leah flipped through the TV channels to find something to amuse Ethan, I read over the itinerary I had been given. I was astonished to see exercise, nutrition and laughter classes, field trips, and prayer time scheduled among Ethan's doctor appointments. Soon a pretty, young volunteer came to give us a tour of the hospital and grounds, her confident, serene voice soothed my strained nerves as she led us through the halls. We walked into the dining room and the first thing to see was a large mural of Dr. Contreras wrestling the zodiac Crab "Cancer" covering the entire length of the wall.

I believed we were in the right place. The buffet table was covered with organic, whole foods. Vegetables were mounded high on platters, bowls of large salads with pureed vegetable dressings to the side. A special table was clearly marked "Gerson Diet Patients" for those that were to follow the Gerson recommended food combinations. The aide took time to explain to us the founding principle of the Gerson therapy and how chronic disease in the body is the result of the toxicity of our food, water, air, and the environment and the lack of enough whole food nutrition.

My mind began to whirl. A completely new world was opening to me. Our tour guide was speaking a method of health I was desperate to learn and understand. I no longer felt like a solitary soldier facing an indomitable army. She explained how the Oasis program teaches the importance of diligently avoiding GMOs (genetically modified organisms), artificial, processed chemical foods and how to detoxify and support the body so it could heal. She reiterated the importance of only consuming fresh, raw, nutrient-rich plant foods in their natural state. She sternly instructed how imperative it was that we adhere to the set juicing regime in order to alkalize Ethan's body.

She warned us that cancer thrives in low oxygen and high acidic conditions. The girl further explained that an acidic state would lead to a decrease in oxygen in the cells and that an airless condition hosts a plethora of other pathogens as well and complicates the cancer treatment. My mind raced over the list of parasites, viruses, and bacteria that were detected through the electoral dermal screening that Ethan had and it all made sense to me.

The next day I met with Dr. Contreras. He explained that although the diagnosis was not favorable for Ethan, we should remain very hopeful for there was still much that we could do. I felt that I finally grasped enough of what was happening in Ethan's body to trust the procedures being recommended. I learned a new term—homeostasis. We were going to bring balance to Ethan's body by addressing every aspect of his imbalance. This included Ethan's physical, mental, spiritual, emotional, and nutritional needs.

Dr. Contreras outlined the schedule for tests and explained what they would be looking for. I noticed that many of the tests would be the same as those that had been done at the children's hospital but with a much different intention. They would use the information to find out what healing process could be stimulated using the body's natural means, as well as to incorporate crucial medications and measures to maintain Ethan's blood counts until the body could detoxify and heal.

I began to wonder why it was so much easier for people to trust medical intervention using chemicals created by man than a process that uses natural remedies made by God for our healing. I was even learning that for much of the manmade chemical toxicity in the world, there were natural solutions, ones provided by God ahead of time, to remedy the insult on the body.

The place for lifesaving surgery and medications for critical care is undeniable, but what about when disease is the result of toxicity, compromised immune system, and poor nutrition? It became intolerable to me that it was not commonplace for the medical and integrative communities to work together.

Questions plagued me. I wondered why more medical doctors in my own country seemed to resist embracing a holistic attitude. What was the disconnect? I was a working single mom learning these principles and embracing alternative ways to healing. What was preventing medical doctors with a decade or more of higher learning from understanding what I had managed to grasp? Why were they not collaborating more with those who practice integrative, whole body healing so more people everywhere would have access to this information and treatment?

If there were such facilities as Oasis close to home, why was it so difficult to find them? I was learning that all the parts of our bodies are interdependent. Why do not all healing communities work together? Why were they not more concerned about the body's pathways of connectedness and how each system depended on and communicated with the other? Surely, there must be a better way to more efficiently run the current healthcare system to allow people greater access with more coverage from their medical insurance. I curtailed my thoughts knowing it would only fuel my frustration.

I knew from experience that in order to reserve my energy I needed to focus on what lay immediately before me. Turning my attention to the next thing on the agenda, I headed to the hospital kitchen for a juicing class to learn the purpose and power of dark-green leafy vegetables to help detoxify and build healthy cells. I watched as the instructor fed fresh, green vegetables into the juicing machine. I was enthralled as it pulverized and squeezed the produce, separating the fiber, releasing its liquid and nutrients into a glass. Optimistically skeptical, I hoped they would offer a way to successfully get the very green elixir into my six-year-old son's body.

When I read the order that Ethan was to go outside for exercise and fresh air frequently each day, I was astounded. Once again, I found myself attempting to "unlearn" all I had been told and had experienced at the children's hospital back home. For weeks at a time, we had been isolated and quarantined during his treatments there. Still, determined and committed to our new path, I carried Ethan down to the entrance of the hospital. The doorman, Augustine, smiled at us in greeting and held the door open as I stepped outside and took a deep breath. I took one hesitant step, then settled on the ledge of the retaining wall. I rocked Ethan on my lap as the sun warmed my skin. Cherishing the feeling of holding him in my arms, I tried to stay in the present moment, resisting the memory of failures tempting to lure me into the past and the uncertainty of the future.

> "Forget the former things; do not dwell on the past. See, I am doing a new thing! Now it springs up; do you not perceive it? I am making a way in the desert and streams in the wasteland" (Isa. 43:18–19, NIV).

Each day we ventured a few steps further and further. First, to a small patio past the entrance, to play with a red ball that Augustine had found for us. Then, to the end of the block, where we could see the large bullfighting arena. When Sunday arrived, I received a note that there was a Catholic Church within walking distance and our wandering finally found a purpose.

I gently picked up Ethan's slight body and I draped him over my back, linking his arms together with one of my hands. I crossed my other arm behind my back, supporting him by slipping my fingers into the loop of my jeans to hold him secure. "Are you ready for our adventure today?" I asked him over my shoulder, smiling at his enthusiastic nod. Leaving his sister in our room to surf the meager television channels, we set off. She had lost interest in what had now become our daily trek downtown to mass, and I didn't have any reserve energy to insist that she come.

After walking five blocks, I welcomed the numbness that crept down my arm as I shifted Ethan's weight to keep him from sliding off my back. If I had to, I would have crawled the rest of the way to be nearer to Jesus in the Eucharist and the comfort I found there. The very thought of Him there, waiting for me in a very real way, kept my feet from stopping. Climbing the last few steps to the church, I felt the last of my strength give way. I carefully laid Ethan on the pew nearest to the entrance, slid in beside him and then to my knees.

The mass soon began and I stood, my legs shaking from the effort. Relief and gratitude for the Universal Catholic Church filled my heart. My eyes stung with tears as I easily followed the Spanish liturgy without knowing the language. Each memorized prayer that I now mouthed along in English, brought strength back into my body. It transported my spirit to the safety and comfort of being at the same altar, surrounded by the same prayers, prayed by my own family and community back home.

Ethan soon regained enough strength to finally begin the intravenous therapies. His late evening infusion had barely begun when his weak cry woke me where I had dozed off, asleep in the chair. "I'm cold. I'm cold!" the words were blurted out between his chattering teeth. I heard his bed tapping against the wall as tremors racked his body so badly they shook the entire bed he was lying on. Calling out to wake my daughter who lay asleep across the room, I pounded on the nurse call-button, praying to God someone was out there listening. "Climb into the bed next to him!" I cried, as I quickly did the same. We pressed his frail body closely between us hoping the warmth from our bodies would stop his shaking. His teeth chattered uncontrollably, and I pressed my cheek against his, holding his jaw gently in my hand.

Speaking with surprising calm, my lips close to his ear, I prayed in Jesus's name, commanding every muscle, bone, tissue organ, cell and system in his body to come into alignment with the Word of God and to perform to the perfection for which it was created. Vaguely, I was aware of the commotion around us. I understood enough with my high school Spanish to know that help was on its way as I heard, "El médico esta llegando!" For interminable moments, we held onto Ethan, vigorously rubbing his limbs, until the solution injected into his IV began to lessen the intense detoxification reaction, and Ethan became still and placid in our arms.

*****

"Put me down!" Ethan demanded as I carried him down the aisle of the plane to disembark. Tears of joy came to my eyes as I watched him run ahead to grab the hand of his sister. Less than thirty days earlier, I had carried Ethan on the plane with no life in him. Now I could barely contain my son in his newfound energy as he ran off the plane. It was miraculous.

I allowed myself to savor the elation until settled at home and the next step loomed ahead of me. I understood that I needed a medical doctor nearby, a pediatric hematologist oncologist to oversee Ethan's blood counts. I sat on the kitchen barstool with the phone book on my lap in front of me and simply prayed, "Lord, please lead me," as I dialed. The physician referral receptionist who answered suggested a doctor I could try at the Catholic Children's Hospital in the neighboring state.

When I spoke with the doctor there, I told her that I would be taking Ethan out of the care of the children's hospital where he had been treated and would now be using natural alternative therapies to support my son at this stage of his treatment. Listening patiently to my concerns, she admitted she had not had any specialized training in natural medicine, but she knew many of her families were using homeopathy and nutrition along with their treatment. She frankly stated those kids were often the ones who did better than those who did not. Relieved, I agreed to bring Ethan in to see her. Congruent with the recommendations from Dr. Contreras, she monitored Ethan's progress while I aggressively worked to detox and nourish his body.

I filled every corner of my mind with words of life. I voraciously consumed every book I could find on toxins, cancer, and nutrition. Then I chose—a hundred times every day. I chose what I would think, what I would believe. I chose what I would bring into the house, what food we would eat, always questioning if it was good for us or not. Would it nourish my son's body or further tax its function as he attempted to detoxify and heal? Were my words blessing us or binding us with a curse of unbelief. My thoughts and words were soldiers in the battlefield of my mind, and fighting as if our life depended on it, I was going to consciously choose which words stood strong and which fell to the wayside.

I took responsibility for what I now knew had compounded Ethan's problem—benzene. I was the one who unknowingly had painted my walls with toxic benzene paint and stored the unused portion in the utility room. I had purchased cheap formaldehyde-containing pressboard furniture. I had been feeding my family inexpensive processed convenience foods. Even though I had not known of the dangers and repercussions of those uninformed decisions, my actions had created a problem for my son. I had forgiven myself for my ignorance, but the process of letting it go demanded more. I wanted to use what I had learned and find a way to help prevent others from making the same mistakes.

Ethan held his own as we continued to travel every eight weeks to Texas to monitor his detox. Then nine months into our regiment of herbs, supplements, homeopathy, essential oils, detox baths, and kale green drinks, the word we were waiting for was given. The benzene was removed, and I fully understood it was no coincidence that cancer was no longer detected in his body. Whirling Ethan through the air amidst our shrieks of laughter, I loudly blessed the Lord and then profusely thanked Doug Leber as we danced the happy dance of joy right there in his office.

CHAPTER 8
Generosity

WE'RE ON OUR WAY

We're on our way; can you
see it in our face?
There's a statement we must make
and there's a journey we must take
Across the land, we're all joining in
the band, leaving everything we can
To follow Him, the great I AM.

Take me up, take me high, take
my will, and take my life
Take my hand and I will
fly and learn to soar
Through the tears, without fear
through the clouds and when it clears
They will see in us the glory of the Lord.

On our way, we have passed
from grace to grace

and know the risk that we must take,
to show the difference we can make.
We are young, we are strong,
and we'll hold on
And when the final song is sung
you'll see the victory we have won.

Take me up, take me high, take
my will, and take my life
Take my hand and I will
fly and learn to soar
Through the tears, without fear
through the clouds and when it clears
They will see in us the glory of the Lord.
(Song by Eileen)

While Ethan healed, I continued my own healing journey. In the daytime hours, I was distracted enough with the reopening of the day care. At night, I poured the poison of all we had been through into the hands of God. His touch sieved out the bitterness, and I was left with His peace in its place. There was always something valuable to be learned. There was something from the path our life had taken to be shared. I began to truly and wholeheartedly believe that God would use what was meant for our harm to help others, possibly preventing tragedy in their future. There had to be a way to pass the hope that we had been given onto others.

A vision began to take shape. Looking into the mirror, my eyes staring back at me, I felt as if by sheer will I could peel back the layers of physical appearance of iris and cornea, and somehow see past the soreness of my soul into the depths of my heart. I felt a calling on my life beyond mother and caregiver. I listened intently to what became a deafening silence. I was now intent on gaining some sense of what I should do with what we learned. I felt a burning desire to help parents navigate the road to better health and avoid the pitfalls that created a perfect storm for my son to become ill. What would motivate others to practice the steps I had learned—*before* they experienced such a heart-rending crisis?

The rigorous daily routine of juicing was becoming a strain on our family, and we more than most had reason to remain motivated. It was just plain hard to keep up the juicing, but I knew for Ethan's sake I could not give up. Those thoughts preoccupied my mind as I walked into my family chiropractor's office one day, hoping to alleviate the headaches I had lately developed. After listening patiently to me tell of my exhausting juicing schedule and seeing the toll it was taking on me, my chiropractor asked me to follow him. He took me into his back office and showed me a colorful poster of twenty-six fruits, vegetables, and berries. Then lifting the lids of three bottles on his desk, he placed two green, two red, and two purple capsules in my hand.

"What is this?" I asked.

"Eileen, I know you are doing your best, but I think you could use some help," he said. I expectantly waited for him to explain. "These are vegetable and fruit capsules. Juice Plus+˚ was created by a doctor who wanted to get healing produce into his father who was dying of cancer and with it, his father recovered. The vegetables, fruits, and berries in these capsules have already been juiced and giving them to Ethan would save you a lot of work. I also believe it will help you to know such a large variety of vine-ripened produce will be in Ethan's body every single day. It will help fill in any gaps in Ethan's nutrition, and you will not feel so bad on the days that you feel unable to juice. All my family takes it. It's made a difference for us and I know it will for you too."

> "Behold, I have given you every plant yielding seed that is on the surface of all the earth, and every tree which has fruit yielding seed; it shall be food for you" (Gen. 1:29, NASB).

I stared down at the green, red, and purple capsules. In disbelief, I reached for the bottles in his hand. In turning each one, I read the list of all the fruit, vegetables, and berries that were contained in each bottle. Could this be right? Why had no one told me about this before? We had been at a major children's research hospital for four years and no one ever mentioned it.

I thought of how sick Ethan had become taking the chemotherapy and how at times he would barely eat a single bite of food at a time. Why was this not the first approach offered to help get life-giving produce into his body instead of the dead chemical concoction in a can that the doctor recommended? The tears that I struggled to keep at bay sharply stung my eyes as a wave of hope washed over me. I read the bottle. It did not have a supplement label—I was looking at a nutrition label. I got that now. I saw that same kind of label on the bag of spinach and apples that I bought and paid a higher price for when I shopped for organic produce to juice each week.

My mind filled with the hours of driving I invested each week to find organic produce. Just thinking about it conjured up the anxiety I had experienced each time I approached the cash register, wondering how I would pull resources from other household expenses to pay for my son's juicing program. I was exhausted from hours of washing produce, juicing, and cleaning the machine, only to begin again. I thought of the emotional toll it was taking on all of us to cajole a seven-year-old into drinking the "magical" green elixir and the myriad of ways we dealt with the ensuing gag response.

Why had I not heard of juiced vegetables in capsules before? And if I had, would I have even understood its importance? I had been forcing Ethan to swallow chemotherapy and prescription medications since he was three years old. He could certainly manage the capsule or chewable form of vegetable and fruit powders. It dawned on me that what I was being handed was a gift beyond price for our family. I was being given an answer to a prayer I had not even known my exhausted heart had been praying and I felt liberated. It was as if a friend just walked in and announced they would relieve me of the stress of ensuring my son would ingest his life-giving greens every day from this day forward. I felt the heavy burden I was carrying lift from my shoulders.

"For your Father knows what you need
before you ask Him" (Matt. 6:8b, NIV).

Would it have been different had I not veered from God's original plan for what He instructed His people to eat in the first place? I certainly had not made feeding my family fresh produce a priority, but with my son, I had living proof of what a difference a conscious effort could make. Planning proper meals had fallen to the bottom of my priority list, beneath providing an income to pay the bills and the never-ending chores and errands of a single mom.

I knew of many people like me who were also struggling to nourish their family. It is difficult for anyone to add even one more thing to the proverbial to-do list, but it becomes mind numbing when your child's life depends on what you do or do not do. With our limited resources, I knew the encapsulated produce solution would save me time and money. It would save me precious energy, and I would still be assured that all those healing fruits and vegetables would be circulating in my son's blood stream, rebuilding, and detoxifying his body each day, even on my busiest days.

Blessing God for His faithfulness, I thanked my chiropractor and asked him if I could buy the bottles I held in my hands. It solved so many of my problems that I wanted it—no matter the cost. He smiled at my eagerness but replied, "We can enroll him in the Juice Plus+ Family Health Study and they will provide his portion at no cost to you when you take it yourself." I was speechless. The impact it would have had on Ethan's depleted body those years he was in treatment would have been immense! The familiar faces of anguished mothers I passed in the halls of the children's hospital loomed in my mind. What an easy way it would have been to help keep our children nourished! Why hadn't I known before? I forced myself to let it go. I knew it now and one thing I knew for sure, it made sense to me.

I sat at the desk filling out the Family Health Study forms amazed at what this would mean for us. All at once, I was startled with an inner nudging, "Feed my lambs." The words flashed across my mind like a banner and drew my attention upward to the fruit and vegetable chart on the doctor's office wall. I recognized that I had heard those same words spoken to me while praying at the Cabrini Shrine in Colorado nearly a decade earlier. The shrine was one of the stops our youth group made while on our pilgrimage in 1993 to see Pope John Paul II in Denver.

It was in that shrine that the Holy Spirit had called me to nourish the teenagers of our youth group with experiences of God's presence in our *Life Teen* program with those same words. "Feed my lambs." I was hearing the same directive again. Now the words held a deep and literal meaning for me. We had paid the price of childhood disease and had paid dearly. I could no longer ignore the truth. Too many of the children my son had made friends with at the children's hospital had since passed away. Something needed to be done. A massive action was necessary to stop illness and disease from stealing the life away from God's children, and I knew I was being called to be part of it.

"My people are destroyed from lack
of knowledge" (Hos. 4:6, NIV)

I now fully understood that feeding children whole, vine-ripened nutritious food was nonnegotiable. They both needed and deserved to be fed right. I hadn't been paying attention and paid the consequences. I understood that God created the food that was necessary for the bodies He created to heal, the way He created them to heal. Real whole food should have been our only food.

There was a food deception that was infiltrating the homes of busy families like ours, and it was affecting how we were feeding our children. Priorities were skewed and at too high of a price. It was a very real battle, and I was prepared now to fight to win. Armed with a simple solution such as vegetables in a capsule would help increase the odds of getting excellent, consistent, nutrients into the growing bodies of children everywhere. I knew it was a message I needed to share.

Initially, I had difficulty accepting that our children needed to be protected from the toxicity of their world. I lived through the pain of trying to grasp the extent of harm that had been caused by my ignorance to a very real threat. I could hardly bear to think of the repercussions had we not learned to flood my son's body with nutrients, clean up our personal environment and begin regulating those things that were in our control.

"Please test your servants for ten days:
Give us nothing but vegetables to eat and
water to drink . . . At the end of the ten days

they looked healthier and better nourished
than any of the young men who ate the royal
food" (Dan. 1: 12 and 15, NIV).

I was learning that the problem with the Standard
American Diet (SAD) was that it was much like the "royal
food" I read about in Scripture. It may look or smell appetiz-
ing, but it leaves us sick and weak. Many of us were becoming addicted to chemical, convenience, food-like products
and were out of touch with how unhealthy we were becoming as a result. Even so, my family had learned to grasp the
concept of healing foods, all those foods that were missing
from our diet. We were now aware of the things we needed
to avoid and what we needed to add. It had become as simple as making better, healthier choices each time we made a
meal. Our health had become our family hobby, and I knew
if we could learn to do it then others could too.

"Each of you should use whatever gift
you have received to serve others, as faithful stewards of God's grace in its various
forms" (1 Pet. 4:10, NIV).

I decided to join the mission to inspire healthier
living and the first thing I did was to have a discussion
with the moms of the children in my day care. I wanted
every child I knew to be taking Juice Plus+° to help provide nutritional insurance (*more information or ordering at*
www.wholefoodsforkids.com). They all readily agreed they
found it difficult to get their families to eat enough vege-

tables and to eat a variety every day. My solution became theirs as well.

It only took that one conversation to find what I had been searching for—a way to help others. I wanted to share what my family had learned on our journey. I began encouraging other moms to look closely at what they fed their family and to read the labels on things they brought into their homes. Many were surprised at the dangers lurking in their children's favorite snacks. The goal became to provide foods with no labels, foods that were locally grown by organic farmers and better yet, grown ourselves.

I cautioned against continuing to use and consume products with ingredients known to cause cancer while relying on a hope and a prayer to keep them well. I made it a habit to pass along articles I came across that warned of the dangers of chemicals lurking in personal body products and our food supply and the importance of using air and water filters. Discovering how companies were spending millions to create brand loyalty, we needed to ask ourselves if we were making a conscious decision because we wanted the ingredients listed in our body or were we simply buying a brand out of habit. With every dollar we were spending, we were either investing in our wellness or subsidizing an illness. Unlike my crisis-inspired transformation, for most, changes could be made one small step at a time while researching and learning more along the way.

"Or do you not know that your body
is a temple of the Holy Spirit who is in
you, whom you have from God, and that

you are not your own?" (1 Cor. 6:19, NIV).

I learned the basics needed for health are often the very things neglected especially when life becomes stressful and busy yet that is exactly when we need them the most. It is wise to make changes before we find ourselves in a crisis. I have also found it is easier to commit to a new direction when reminding ourselves *why* we are doing it.

One of our most basic needs is clean water. Generally, drinking half our body weight *in ounces* of purified water ensures that the lymph system will have the fluid it needs to flush toxins from the body. The amount we drink can be easily measured to see if we should be drinking more. It is important to use a top-quality water filter to avoid chemicals in the municipal water system because without a water filter the body itself becomes the filter for toxins. A noticeable difference can be felt once we are properly hydrated, and it can cause an improvement in energy, in our mood, and in our ability to concentrate. Filtered water is an easy remedy to reach for when experiencing a headache or muscle pain. When exercising or drinking caffeine or alcohol, there is a need to increase the amount of water we consume even more.

Every cell in the body needs oxygen to perform its functions. Our bodies need fresh, clean air, and mindful breathing is important especially during stressful times. Having an air cleaner and plenty of air-purifying houseplants in the home and office will increase air quality by reducing the amount of exposure to toxic outgassing furniture, office equipment and other household pollutants

(NASA recommends one plant for every one hundred square feet of space). The fewer toxins we inhale, the less stress is put on our detoxifying organs.

Our health depends on real whole food, every day, every meal. Avoiding harmful GMOs, pesticides, herbicides, preservatives, and harmful dyes on and in our food is crucial when choosing which foods to buy. Consuming nutritious, fresh, local vine-ripened organic produce and whole foods provides the correct fuel our bodies need to function properly. The key for prevention of disease is eating the vegetables that create an alkaline environment inhospitable to a host of parasites, viruses, bacteria, and cancer cells. Antioxidants in vegetables, fruit and berries provide cells with the protection, energy, and support needed to continually balance, detoxify, and heal our bodies.

Moving is exercise. Besides burning calories and releasing feel good endorphins, committing to daily exercise moves the lymph system that carries away toxins. It aids the body's detoxifying pathways, especially when we sweat. Sweating is invaluable to detoxification and it is important to keep the skin free from chemical body products that clog the pores. A daily twenty- to thirty-minute walk, preferably outdoors but even on a small rebounder, can do wonders for our mood and overall health. Exercise helps to build muscle strength and flexibility. It will increase circulation and oxygen and positively affect brain function and mental health.

The areas of energy that surround our electronic devices are a serious threat to our health. When the electric current flows, differences in voltage and magnetic fields are created and adversely react to our own electric and bio-chemical responses. We reduce our exposure by unplugging and distancing ourselves from our electronics whenever possible. They are especially harmful to our children's growing brains and pregnant women should use them with extreme caution. We heal while we sleep, so keeping electronics out of the bedroom is imperative to protect us from the EMFs (electromagnetic fields) that harm our cells and disrupt our sleep cycles. EMF protectors and harmonizers can do much to minimize the damage.

As I learned in my healing prayer, issues from trauma early in our life can leave us bound to unwanted thinking patterns and negative habits and actions. If we make the effort to think God's thoughts, take time to study the Scriptures, and pray for God's help, it results in less stress and greater peace. Commitment to one simple change at a time can result in a lifetime of reward. I had all the impetus to change but it still took my commitment to make it happen. Seeking and receiving God's healing and help made it possible for me to take the action necessary to create a healthier lifestyle for my family.

"It is God who arms me with strength and makes my way perfect. He makes my feet like the feet of a deer; he enables me to stand on the heights. He trains my hands for battle; my arms can bend a bow of bronze. You give me your shield of victory, and your right hand sustains me; you stoop down to make me great. You

broaden the path beneath me, so that my
ankles do not turn." (Ps. 18:32–36, NLT)

I was quickly developing a burning passion to share
what I had learned. To me, it would mean the kind of passion from the Latin *pati,* "to suffer, to endure." The path
that I had chosen would become a love that often hurt
because many were not ready to hear the message. My
heart was so invested in helping others avoid the threats to
developing cancer that I was surprised at how often I was
met with disinterest and sometimes even hostility. Even
my own mother responded with disbelief to my newfound
information. "Well, if it was not safe, the store would not
sell it, would they?" she asked, bewildered. My research
revealed that to be far from the truth.

It was easier to understand objections to making a
change to unhealthy habits, when I stopped to consider
how it took me the experience of nearly losing my son to
change our own lifestyle. I knew it was grace that enabled
me to start searching for an answer "outside the box" when
I did and to change my thinking. I would trust that God
would inspire others to as well.

I had to let go of the sense of guilt I felt when I connected the dots between the toxin benzene that I unwit-
tingly allowed in our home, and its documented correlation
to the incidence of childhood leukemia. I knew personally
the pain of regret learning that my three-year-old's favorite
foods, the lunchmeat and hotdogs that I fed him regularly,
were filled with cancer-causing nitrites. Not wanting to

offend but still feeling a responsibility to share what I had learned, I prayed for sensitivity when sharing our story.

Nevertheless, I remained undaunted. Without apology, I would share what I had learned. I would prepare myself as best I could, make a plan, and depend on God to arrange divine appointments with those who needed this information as desperately as I had. I continually saw myself in the eyes of the young moms who crossed my path. What would *our* story have looked like if *I* had learned the life-saving benefits of whole food nutrition sooner? I quickly realized there was no grace in maintaining regrets, and I looked forward to the new direction my life was taking. I understood not all would receive my message, but it was one that needed to be shared.

> "Great peace have those who love your law, and nothing can make them stumble" (Ps. 119:165, NIV).

I was not afraid of what people would think of me when I first began sharing our story. However, I realized I *was* afraid of missing someone the Lord was sending my way, someone who was praying for a solution to his or her health challenge. I became more mindful of those who crossed my path. I began to pray I would meet those who would benefit from hearing about our journey and who desired to learn how they might prevent a health crisis by implementing what I had learned. I knew that eating the recommended servings of fresh produce was a worthwhile goal, but many families consistently had a hard time achieving it every day. Those I met would know there was a helpful solution for them as well if they wanted it.

Hippocrates, considered by many to be the father of medicine, said, "A wise man should consider that health is the greatest of human blessings and learn how to, by his own thought, derive benefit from his illnesses." Seeing a need and trying to fill it, I began to share what I had learned at every opportunity. I was asked to give "kitchen consultations" to family and friends who wanted help to clean up and "green" their personal environment, and I did what I could to help them. I taught the dangers of the top ten household toxins like benzene and endocrine disrupting phalates and how to read labels to avoid harmful chemicals. I introduced them to natural and effective soaps and cleaners such as vinegar, baking soda, and essential oils.

When I was met with resistance when sharing the dangers of electromagnetic fields and radiation from microwaves, cell phones, smart meters, and other electronic devices it was usually because of someone's dependence on the convenience of the technology. Even though there were an increasing number of families that were opting out of a system that has created this stress on our bodies, it is not an option for many. However, for the very ill, the sacrifice is worth the benefits.

Once the ingredients on labels are understood, it is easier to remove toxic household products from the home. It was imperative to read the labels of cleaners, shampoo, soaps, cosmetics, personal hygiene, and baby care products, avoiding air fresheners, paraffin candles, bug sprays, lawn pesticides, and insecticides. There was wisdom in reaching first for natural food remedies for colds such as garlic, ginger, raw local organic honey, and fermented foods. There were endless benefits of drinking raw organic apple cider vinegar and using baking soda for digestive upsets and to help alkalize the body and turmeric for pain relief.

I assisted mothers in purging their pantries of packaged products with colors, dyes, preservatives, and other additives once they learned how those things negatively affected their children's health. I taught them how to shop the perimeter of the grocery store for live whole foods and how to make it a game they can play with their children. The first items in the cart were to be fresh organic vegetables and fruit and berries, seeds, beans, nuts, and coconut oil. For those not vegetarian, raw local dairy and honey, wild caught fish, and grass-fed organic eggs and meats were added. We met head on the obstacles to changing unconscious shopping habits and ingrained food beliefs.

My whole food Juice Plus+° solution became indispensable to those who were learning to nourish themselves again. Without a personal experience of crisis, there often was not the motivation to make a complete lifestyle change overnight as I did. Families would be able to get fruit, vegetable, and berry powders into their bloodstream immediately, gaining the benefits of better nutrition while learning practical ways to eat healthier. I had been given a way to use what I had learned and in turn had found a way to serve.

"God is not unjust; he will not forget your work and the love you have shown him as you have helped his people and continue to help them" (Heb. 6:10, NIV).

CHAPTER 9
Faithfulness

MY FOREVER FRIEND

I have a friend sent from heaven.
My prayer has been heard and answered.
It's so obvious you know.
You know what's best for me,
it's how it ought to be.
No matter how I disagree.
My spirit leads me to the faith I have
in you and I'd do anything for you.
I have a friend sent from heaven.
My prayer has been heard and answered.
You see me as I really am. You recog-
nize in me the child I long to be.
And if the world does not
agree, you will protect me.
It's how I want it to be, you
always here for me.
I have a friend sent from heaven.
My prayer has been heard and answered.

Promise me, tell me once again that you
love me as I am, my forever friend.
I have a friend sent from heaven.
My prayer has been heard and answered.
It's as if every lonely hour
I've spent in prayer,
wondering if someone on this earth
would ever care, has brought you here.
(Song by Eileen)

I was on a journey to reach my heart's desire although I did not realize it at the time. God's hand was orchestrating people and events in a way that I could never have conceived, and I know it would not have occurred any other way. God understands our motives, hearts, and history. He answers our prayers while at the same time accomplishing His purpose.

When I become impatient, I often imagine a timeline spread out in front of me as far as the eye can see. I trust that God has heard me and what I have prayed will be answered. I can visualize the hand of God placing what I have prayed for, or something far better for me, somewhere on that timeline, and I am filled with hope and certainty. It gives me a sense of peace knowing that I do not have to know how, when, or where God will answer my prayer. I can be assured that He is faithful to His promises and He knows how to provide in a way that will be for my good even amidst great loss.

Although I had not yet been born and did not personally experience the day my brother Joey died, I was profoundly affected by the feelings and the stories surrounding his death. Even those things that had no explanation as to why they happened still work to our good when God speaks into them. I know that experiencing my story in the light of Christ, *affirmed by the Word of God*, has affected every area of my life. It helped to form the part of me that believes that all children are precious and that they are a great gift to be treasured. It helped me to become a woman who would love having children of her own, one who would love to help care for others' children as well.

> "'For I know the plans I have for you,'
> declares the Lord, 'Plans to prosper you
> and not to harm you, plans to give you a
> hope and a future'" (Jer. 29:11, NIV).

I have seen God change things in me that I was unable to change on my own. I have experienced His peace in circumstances that should have given me torment and pain. Purposefully acknowledging and thanking God for each blessing have made me increasingly aware of all the good things He provides for me daily. I have become more mindful of the events that God orchestrates to bring about the answer to my prayers, including the cooperation of many other hearts as well as my own.

> "And behold, this day I am going the
> way of all the earth. Know in all your hearts
> and in all your souls that not one thing
> has failed of all the good things which the

Lord your God promised concerning you.
All have come to pass for you; not one
thing of them has failed" (Joshua 23:14).

The wait was over. It was finally spring, and given any
opportunity, I escaped the house for hours at a time expanding my gardens. I prayed while I weeded, digging up and
transplanting my plants as they multiplied and spilled over
their borders. It was one of my favorite private places where
I felt closest to God. As I ripped the invasive thistle from
between the pavers in the flagstone path, I knew it was time
and I could envision His skilled hand extracting the thorny
hedge I'd erected to protect myself from feeling the pain of
what we had been through. I happily discarded the weeds
while at the same time allowing God to prune away any
tangled parts of my thinking and restore order. I longed for
and welcomed His touch on every aspect of my life.

I vividly remember the warmth of the sun that day
as I sat on a tree stump separating my overgrown hosta
plants. I felt a heightening sense that someone was coming.
The feeling was so strong that I looked up and stared at
the corner of my house expectantly waiting for someone
to appear. Although I saw no one, much to my surprise, I
realized I no longer feared what was coming in my future.
In fact, I greatly anticipated what it would be. Suddenly, I
wanted to feel something new and exciting again. I knew
Ethan was getting stronger every day. Being less distracted
with his care, I felt my heart begin to beat with yearning
to be with someone special. I had grown to depend on the
Lord for comfort and companionship and He never dis-

appointed. Yet there was a new space opening within my heart that I didn't intend and felt no desire to stop.

I felt God's presence there in my garden, encouraging me. He was showing me how He had taken each experience in my life and used it to demonstrate His love for me. The access I had given Him to my heart allowed Him to mold me into someone who could love and be loved. I began to understand that the work He had done and was doing in me was a necessary part of that preparation process. I knew God was powerfully at work in me, and I even sensed though I still managed to fail daily, He was pleased with me.

The practice of rejecting the doubts that threatened to undermine my confidence in God's love and approval had made me stronger. I realized that I now fully believed I am "a child of God" (Rom. 8:16), "forgiven" (Col. 1:13–14), "sanctified" (1 Cor. 6:11), "redeemed" (Ps. 107:2), "blessed" (Deut. 28:6), "healed" (1 Pet. 2:24), "saved by grace through faith" (Eph. 2:8), "a new creature" (2 Cor. 5:17), "led by the Spirit of God" (Rom. 8:14), "free from all bondage" (John 8:36), "strong in the Lord" (Eph. 6:10), "able to do all things in Christ" (Phil. 4:13), "an heir of God" (Rom. 8:17), and "light to the world" (Matt. 5:14).

Continually restored by God's truth, I was now becoming sensitive to the good things that He wanted me to have, even when I felt I had evidence that I did not deserve them. I believed that God would reward the work I had done, and I wanted to see Him praised for all He had accomplished through the changes He had made in me. I felt compelled to pray to become someone who would attract a man who was also seeking the heart of the Father.

> "And without faith it is impossible to
> please Him, for he who comes to God must
> believe that He is and that He is a rewarder
> of those who seek Him" (Heb. 11:6, NASB).

By midsummer, we were experiencing unusually hot temperatures. I breathed a sigh of relief as I stepped into the shower after a challenging ten hours in the day care. I began to send up a prayer of thanksgiving that I had been able to finally purchase an air-conditioning unit for our home, while trying not to think of the impending increase it would make to my electric bill. Ignoring the ringing phone, as best as I could, I was startled when the receiver was thrust into the shower and dropped at my feet. "It's for you," my eight-year-old son declared and then slammed the door on his way out.

"Wait!" I hollered in a futile attempt to stop him. I snatched up the phone before it was drenched. Aggravated, I brusquely clipped, "Hello?"

"Hello! This is David Albrecht. We met at your recent Juice Plus+° Health Event!" the cheerful voice announced.

I remembered the naturopathic doctor who had brought my business sponsor into the business, from meetings I had attended in the past. The inconvenient interruption grated on my last nerve as the man announced he was giving me a courtesy call.

Incensed, I said, "I'm sorry, but this is not really a good time to talk!"

"All right then, I'll be brief." With considerable enthusiasm, Dr. Albrecht proceeded to explain how he noticed that I was falling short of my business qualification for the month and that I would be leaving (truthfully, much needed!) money on the table. He then offered to help me make sure that I met the promotional deadline before the close of business the next day.

I responded with a stream of excuses that flowed more hotly than the water from my increasingly tepid shower. "I hope you can understand that this is not a good time to talk. I just finished ten hours working in my day care. I homeschool my daughters and care for twelve other children all week. Please believe me when I say I have enough on my plate right now. As you know, my son is recovering from a long illness and Juice Plus+° has been a godsend for us. Although I will continue to share it with other moms, I am just not interested in anything more."

He calmly replied, "Okay, I see. That's fine. You are sure to help a few people along the way and that's fine. If you are happy with what you are making, that's fine. I just wanted to offer my assistance in case you wanted to help even more people than you are now. Although it's true that it's possible to earn substantially more by helping more people, many are happy with earning just 'a little something extra' each month, and that's fine."

At that point, the steam coming from the shower had nothing to do with the temperature of the water. Who was this person? Why were we having this conversation? In fact,

I was counting the minutes in pennies, while the wasted water of my precious shower ran unused down the drain. It flitted through my mind, that at that moment, I would like to make him eat his "little something extra." Piqued and wanting to end the call, I took the man's invitation to the next training as a personal challenge and to my own astonishment, agreed to attend.

A few months later, I was pleased with myself at the effect his unsolicited call provoked. I arrived at my first "boot camp" training weekend with my growing team. Proving God can work through unique personalities, I reluctantly admitted I had swallowed the bait—hook, line, and sinker. At first, I was exasperated with David Albrecht for assuming I was okay with just earning "a little something extra." I knew what I really wanted was to give mothers a way to increase their children's nutrition, to help prevent childhood disease and to avoid a crisis like the one we had experienced. I had let the business of life stop me from pursuing what really mattered to me. I no longer cared how God had gotten me to the training. I was grateful to be there.

At the event the first evening, I heard firsthand stories from people like me who saw dramatic changes when they started taking Juice Plus+°. I was seeing on a larger scale, that I was not alone in my struggle to provide enough life-giving, plant nutrition for my family and I heard how grateful so many were to have found such a simple solution.

The next day, a panel of expert doctors began answering specific questions about the quality of produce used in our product, where and how it was grown, and about the exceptional quality and variety of gold standard, double blind, placebo-controlled studies that were done at universities and medical centers around the world. I became increasingly confident that God was leading me on this path and I felt my vision growing.

I tried to pay attention when Dr. Albrecht shared the benefits that athletes in his practice experienced on Juice Plus+® but instead was distracted by his good humor and inexplicably drawn to his powerful runner's thighs. I was relieved when the meeting concluded, and we were free to spend the afternoon enjoying the lake.

Floating in the clear cool water did wonders to calm my nerves. My mind wandered to all the things going well in my life. I was happy with my flourishing day care, enjoying my friends and family and blessed with Ethan's returning health. So why was I so irritated earlier when David Albrecht introduced me to the friend he had brought with him . . . what was her name . . . that other blonde? Before I could stew over my annoyance any further, my thoughts were interrupted with the reminder of the prayer I had said in my garden the previous spring "to meet someone special." My swimming companions and I began to head to shore just as the cause of my discomfort sauntered down to the dock to inform us that dinner was being set out.

"You won't want to miss this feast. It looks delicious!" He announced, then gallantly reached down to assist me out of the water. Becoming possessed with the mischief of a schoolgirl, I yanked his outstretched arm and managed to send him flying, fully dressed, headlong over my shoulder, into the lake.

After the initial splash I cringed, momentarily mortified, at what I had just done. I had just sent a respected doctor, a National Marketing Director who was part of a multimillion-dollar company, plunging into the lake. I had experienced more than my fair share of my brothers' swimming pool dunkings in my life and briefly wondered at all the possible repercussions of this one.

Climbing quickly onto the shore, I paused in my escape to glance over my shoulder to see David's reaction. He surfaced the water sputtering and looked up in surprise. David caught sight of me fleeing, then threw his head back and laughed. Shrugging in feigned indifference, I abruptly turned and scampered up the hill and away. I tried unsuccessfully to ignore the guilt of leaving him there drenched, shaking out the soaked, and probably ruined, contents of his wallet.

A year would pass before I would again be confronted with my attraction to the friendly, free-spirited David Albrecht. Something had been awakened in me at our last encounter, and I eagerly looked forward to seeing him again. I had been single for eleven years. My focus had interminably and rightfully been on taking care of my family, but now I was seriously considering the possibility of more.

I thought I had already sufficiently expressed my interest in David but now wondered if the dunk in the lake had been too subtle. I admitted that my approach may have been influenced by the exasperating phone call I had received from him that fateful day while in the shower. There was no doubt that David had ignited my competitive spirit and had roused me to change directions in my life instead of flowing with the current to wherever my busy life led me. His challenge left me burning to flex my muscles and swim against the tide to go where I wanted to go in life. After all, why not? I was an excellent swimmer.

Not much had changed, but me, when the annual boot camp rolled around the following year. Once again, the temperature was rising and reached ninety degrees by mid-afternoon. This time I was anticipating the fun and training at the Juice Plus+ boot camp up north. Hoping there would be a respite from the heat with the cooler temperatures common for northern Michigan, I quickly threw together the barest of essentials, anxious to be on my way. Waving to the last of the day-care kids as their parents pulled out of my driveway, I climbed into the truck with my Juice Plus+ sponsor Dr. Jim Hubbard, and we headed north straight up Interstate-75.

We arrived at the camp just past midnight. Dr. Jim and I walked out onto the deserted dock to stretch our legs and admire the clear lake sparkling in the moonlight. David Albrecht, hearing of our arrival, came down and warmly greeted us. I was not dressed for the dipping northern temperature and soon was shivering in the capris and tank top I still wore from work that day. Turning to go pick up my jacket and bag from the car, I paused in my tracks when I heard David explain to Jim that he had come alone to the boot camp this year. I inwardly smiled and changing my direction, found myself next to Jim just as his cell phone slipped out of his hand, and splashed into the water. Both

232

men stared as the phone began sinking beneath the surface. Without thinking twice, I jumped in after it.

Retrieving the phone and handing it up to Jim, I laughed in triumph when he announced that it still worked. This time, I sincerely smiled when David reached down to assist me. I took his hand as I climbed back up onto the dock. David invited us to stop over to his motorhome to end the night with a drink and I set off to change into dry clothes. Upon returning, I found our little party had increased in size. I settled in to enjoy the company and the precious time I had without any children at my knees.

One by one, all those who had joined the gathering began leaving to turn in. In no hurry to end the evening, David and I were the last to remain. I listened as he spoke quite poetically about the search to discover the heart's desire. He shared his insights on how the quest to follow the heart was a lifelong journey and how our hearts reveal what we are called to do if we would listen. Pointedly, he asked me, "So what's in your heart, Eileen? If your heart could talk, what would it say?" Looking up from my Pellegrino and lime, my gaze direct, I said quite unexpectantly, "I just want to be kissed."

We looked intently at each other for a moment before he thoughtfully replied, "I would do that for you." At my nod, he rose from his seat across the table and slid onto the bench beside me. When I left for my dorm room moments later, I decided that even if that were to be all I took home from the weekend, it was well worth the trip.

"Remember how the Lord your God
led you all the way in the desert these forty
years, to humble you and to test you in
order to know what was in your heart,
whether or not you would keep his commands. He humbled you . . . to teach you
that man does not live by bread alone but
on every word that comes from the mouth
of the Lord." (Deut. 8:2–3, ISV)

Parting that weekend, David asked to see me again
when he came through town, which began happening with
regularity. We soon found we both thoroughly enjoyed
each other's company. It was rapidly feeling better for me
to be with David than apart. Feeling safe and at ease, I
didn't hesitate to accept when he offered to take me to celebrate my nephew's wedding in Virginia.

I learned a lot about David's free spirit as we drove
east, and it was quickly becoming apparent that he was well
traveled and traveled well. I found I was deeply affected
as he shared with me thoughtful stories of his experiences
in Vietnam, and I was delightfully entertained with his
cross-country motorcycle trips and sailing adventures.
Even holding his hand in companionable silence, I felt
more than content.

Tears came to my eyes as I contemplated what a gift I
was being given to have David's company. I was startled by
the thought "this is a good man," as if the words had been
spoken aloud to me. The insight was so foreign to the way
I had thought about relationships in the past that I turned

to look out the window quite overwhelmed and stunned by my happiness. Catching a glimpse of the passing road sign, it was forever etched in my memory that it was on Route 80, at the Trumbell County line, mile marker 206, that I could no longer deny that I had fallen in love with the man by my side.

We found that we also fell easily into each other's lives. Growing up as an only child, David had always wanted brothers and sisters, and I had plenty to share! I wanted someone to work alongside with, to create with, and I was finding that David did as well.

At the first Juice Plus+ conference we attended together in Memphis, David was being honored for achieving the "39 Club" position and an Elton Award for the fastest growing business that year. As his guest, I walked arm in arm with him, down the red-carpet aisle that led into the opulent ballroom. I was awash with delight until I stumbled mid-stride, leaving my slim stilettoed sandal behind us. Mortified to be holding up the reception line, I bent down to quickly snatch up the shoe, only to be stopped as David leisurely reached down and with aplomb slipped it back on my foot to the amusement of those waiting behind us. I felt a flush of warmth in my chest that reached my face and then laughed aloud as I silently prayed, "Really, Lord, was the Cinderella reference really necessary?" I sensed His definitive and emphatic response, "Yes."

The lyrical passages from the Song of Solomon played in my mind as the evening unfolded. For many years, God had been loving me back into wholeness with His patience, generosity and kindness and with gratitude, I continued to receive His healing touch. I was duly impressed with David's success, but I wanted my newfound wisdom to guide me in my decisions, not my old recklessness. That night, David told me that he always committed his business to God with the prayer "Lord, you are the owner of my business. I am just the manager. Thy will be done," then trusted that everything would always work out for the best, no matter what happened. His faith spoke volumes to my heart and I was set on listening.

> "Commit your works to the LORD
> and your plans will be established"
> (Prov. 16:3, NASB).

The town I grew up in lay on the very industrialized Lake Erie. Unbeknownst to me, across the state lay the beautiful harbor town of Grand Haven on Lake Michigan. David told me he had lived the last twenty years there and he was pleased when I agreed to drive over with him to see why he loved it so much. Our first stop there was one of his favorite places on earth. Indicating I should wait, he got out of the car and I smiled, watching him walk around to my side to open my door. He took my hand and I stepped out, stretching my legs and breathing deeply. The grassy dunes were covered in beach grass that swayed in the balmy breeze. The smell of pines hung heavy in the air and I could hear the far-off rush of waves against the shore.

"I want to show you something pretty special," David said, leading us to the head of the walking path.

We moved deeper and deeper through the winding trails of the Rosy Mound Nature Preserve I could feel the tension falling away with each step farther into the pine forest. The air was thick with the scent of fir trees and the musky smell of the fallen leaves. A green canopy parted as we climbed the stairs to the highest point of the dunes. I was struck with awe. The brilliant blue of Lake Michigan stretched before us. White sails dotted the horizon and gently rolling waves, reflecting the brilliant sun, sparkled like a thousand diamonds scattered across the water. I had never seen such a serene place. Holding tightly to his hand I clasped it to my heart and sighed.

Smiling at my delight, he asked, "What do you think?"

"I think we should kiss," I replied.

Turning to him, I prayed he would see the love in my eyes having no words to express my joy. David led me to a bench overlooking the lake. Once seated he became pensive and soon divulged to me that right before we met he had spent a month in the desert in Arizona contemplating his future. It was there that he had reflected on his present state in life, the success of his business and surrendered to whatever the Lord wanted of him. I was amazed at his disclosure, realizing that it was at precisely the same time that I had been praying in my garden, and had sensed that someone was coming.

He told me how he had always envisioned revisiting all the beautiful places he had seen while traveling alone, but with someone special someday. He then told me that he wanted that person to be me. Looking into his eyes, I began to long for the picture he was painting. I felt alive with newfound hope and excitement as I looked at our future together.

With passionate enthusiasm, David shared his journey to becoming a National Marketing Director and how he valued the friends and experiences he gained along the way. As he was speaking, it brought to mind the rare day, long ago, when my dad shared his dream for my life. I had recently come back from my failed attempt to move to Colorado with my girl friend after high school and I was eight months pregnant with my first daughter. Dad had forgiven me for marrying the father of my child against his wishes, although we were both somewhat struggling to come to terms with our changed relationship.

I recalled that I had been visiting my mom when dad came in from work and told me he'd like me to go for a ride with him to meet someone. As we drove along, I listened as Dad told me he had recently become a distributor for a sales company called Shaklee and that we were on the way to meet with his business sponsor. It was the first time I had ever heard of network marketing. He explained how he earned a commission when training others who also wanted to share the health products the company sold, creating a team as well as an additional source of income for our family. When we pulled up to a large house in the suburbs of Detroit, we were greeted by a cheerful couple who warmly welcomed us into their home. I sat quietly to the side while my dad discussed the company's assorted products with the man. The woman asked me if I would like to see the rest of their home, and I followed her down the hallway.

I remembered as we walked through their spacious house, I was drawn to the tasteful décor and fine details of their beautiful home. I had never seen anything like it. She shared her story of how they began sharing their products with friends and family and how their business soon grew to be more than they ever would have dreamed. The woman explained how it had allowed them the financial freedom to travel and to help others in ways they would never have been able without their networking business. Although her story stirred my heart and I thought it was wonderful for her, I did not see how it had anything to do with me.

On the drive home that afternoon, my dad shared with me in a way that he never had before. "Eileen," he began, "I can see you doing this kind of business. I know you are struggling to make ends meet and I believe you could build a business that would provide wonderful things for your family. You could have a home of your own and the ability to travel. You could work from your home, so you could be with your children. If you put your time and effort into this, you would have what you need not only now but in the future."

I knew that Dad was worried about me and the baby. Though my dad's sincerity was evident, his plea fell on deaf ears. To my dad's disappointment, I told him I would think about it. However, I could not conceive it. I did not have it in me to even try.

Now bringing my attention back to David, I began to sense my dad's approval. I clasped David's hand and kissing it, pressed it to my heart. We walked hand in hand across the soft sand of the Lake Michigan beach. I summoned the courage to share with him how many erroneous decisions I had made in the past, and the painful consequences that made me hesitant to ever consider a long-term relationship. David's confidence in me left me speechless. He was not disturbed when I shared my mistakes. He didn't judge me or criticize how I had handled my pain. Every one of David's mature and understanding responses to my admissions drew me deeper. I realized his very presence calmed my restlessness and any doubts.

We left the lakeshore, and I gave David the assurance that I would return with him soon. We committed to spending as much time getting to know each other as possible. The following week we went out to my mom's property to go for a walk together. My brother Donald approached us grasping David's hand in greeting; he commented, "Hey, David, I understand your company used to distribute water filters. Come with me, I want to show you something." We followed Donald to a trailer parked out behind the warehouse. Pushing up the door, he climbed into the trailer and pulled down a large heavy box. Opening it, we gaped at its contents. It was filled with NSA water filters, an earlier product of the Juice Plus+° Company. "There are nine more cases inside here. I guess my dad was part of your company too!" David and I looked at each other in surprise, and we both laughed, sensing my dad's smiling approval.

> "And your ears shall hear a word behind you, saying, 'This is the way, walk in it,' when you turn to the right or when you turn to the left" (Isa. 30:21, NKJV).

CHAPTER 10
Self-Control

"The tongue has the power of
life and death, and those who
love it will eat its fruit."
—Proverbs 18:21 (NIV)

David and I were married on a beautiful summer morning in 2005 surrounded by our family. Everything about our wedding day was the polar-opposite of what I had experienced before. I was eager to learn from the mistakes of my past and the Lord saw to it that I had plenty of comparisons. I was given the gift of arriving at the altar having waited to give ourselves fully to each other within the sanctity of marriage. Both strongly committed, we desired each other's happiness over our own, and we cherished one another. I was David's chosen one, and he was mine.

Everything we had envisioned for our life fell into place, and we were soon moving from my hometown to the beautiful Michigan lakeshore in Grand Haven where we had first begun to build our dream. Buying a home together, we began the work of newlyweds. We were blessed with traveling, making a family of new friends and building our business along the way. Although I missed the fulfillment of a day care full of children, I was now helping moms keep their kids well and it was beyond satisfying to do so.

> "And all things, whatever you shall
> ask in prayer, believing, you shall receive"
> (Matt. 21: 22, KJV).

One summer evening, after a long walk on the beach, David and I sat on the warm sand holding hands awaiting the sunset over the sparkling water of Lake Michigan. We listened with contentment to the gentle lapping as the waves crept up on the sand. It dawned on me then that more than a decade earlier, I had sat on a beach almost directly across this very lake. I was a single mom at that time, on a family vacation visiting friends in Lake Forest, Illinois. I was now living the answered prayer that I had said while building sand castles with my children that day. My hope—to live in such a beautiful place with someone I loved—had been realized.

> "Trust in the LORD with all your heart,
> and do not lean on your own understand-
> ing. In all your ways acknowledge him,
> and He will make straight your paths"
> (Prov. 3:5–6, ESV).

God had indeed restored, confirmed, strengthened, and established me as He had promised (1 Pet. 5:10). As I shared our story of hope and healing, it brought beauty from the ashes of our past and a peaceful rhythm to our new life. My joy felt complete, five years slipping past as effortless as a sail in the wind. Although the only thing certain in life is change, I had no warning for the squall that was about to erupt and abruptly change our course.

Violently jolted from my sleep by a piercing pain, a band of tightness squeezed my chest and I gasped for air. A burning numbness spread across my face and deep tremors wracked my aching legs. I sat up on the side of the bed and gripped the edge of the mattress as a lunging dizziness swept over me. Holding on tightly, I prayed that it would pass, yet I did not believe for a moment that it would. I clung to the dresser as I struggled to my feet and attempted to cross the room. Incredulous, I felt that I needed to find someone to help me before I passed out. I called out for my husband as I made my way along the hall wall clinging to the banister.

Something was wrong. My heart was pounding, I could not think right or speak clearly, and I was beginning to lose the movement in my leg and then my arm. David came quickly and led me into a chair in the living room. Kneeling by my side, he spoke calmly reminding me to breathe deeply. I could only stare blindly at him, his words seeming to echo in my ringing ears. My vision began to blur, and my throat constricted, convincing us of its seriousness. We left quickly for the emergency room.

As soon as we arrived and the tests were ordered, I began admonishing myself for falling back into a broken medical system. It did not add up. I had healthy eating habits, a history of being active, and no history of heart

problems in our family. The battery of tests found no reason for the severe symptoms presented. I was sent home
with a valium pill that I did not take and a bill for several
thousand dollars for our "nonemergency" trip to the ER. I
was living a nightmare.

My life became an exacting experiment of how to
cope with my worsening symptoms. One doctor appointment simply led to two more, none of which resulted in
any diagnosis. I floundered helplessly as I became horribly
incapacitated with no medical explanation for what was
happening. I simply could not understand it. Before I was
fully conscious each morning, I felt the pain cut through
my body, it appeared abruptly, like a breaking shaft of light
dawning on the horizon. My moan reaching my ears before
I could even understand that I was awake.

The unbearable pain left me more exhausted than when
I had fallen asleep. I was dumbfounded that I was somehow still breathing after suffering through the torturous
night. It felt as though the room was tilting before I even
opened my eyes. Once I was conscious, I could not toler-
ate remaining in a prone position for even one moment.
I forced myself up on my elbow, slid from the bed to the
floor, and dragged myself to the bathroom to rest my head
against the cold porcelain tile of the Jacuzzi tub.

Turning on the water faucet just slightly hotter than
I could really stand, I began my prayer, beckoning the
Spirit of God to wash over me and soften the pain that
was coursing through my body like a thousand shards of
broken glass. Seeking relief, I slowly lowered myself as I
did each morning, into the Epsom salt and baking soda

water. I knew I had nothing but a thread of God's grace keeping my head from slipping quietly and forever beneath the water's swirling surface in search of eternal relief. Yet, as tears streamed into the water beneath my chin, I forced air into my aching lungs. Accepting reality, my lips formed the words that then echoed softly off the ceramic tiles that surrounded me, "My God is greater; my God is stronger. God you are higher than any other! My God is healer, awesome in power, my God, my God."

Just moments later, I carefully stepped from the steaming bath, intending to use hot/cold therapy to alter pain signals and force healing by reducing inflammation. Holding fast to the back of a chair, I gingerly reached for the shower door. Bracing myself, I reluctantly turned the faucet to "cold" and cringed as the blast of icy water stung my hot skin. Gasping, I determinedly chanted aloud, "This is good for me. This is good for me!" between chattering teeth.

Leaning on the shower wall for support, I closed my eyes. A vicious image of a thousand sharp needles stabbing my skin filled in my mind. The Name of Jesus crossed my lips and displaced the illusion with a panoramic view of a gentle summer rain beginning to fall softly on a still pond. I moved carefully back to the steaming bath, repeating the process, hot then cold, hot then cold, over and over again, the method working to move my struggling lymph system.

Finally, when I could endure no more, I made my way back to the side of the bed. Lowering myself slowly, I inhaled deeply, each breath more easily expanding my lungs. My body blissfully numb, I found myself in an empty white space of relief, however brief. Determined, I eventually dressed as best I could, shuffled slowly along the wall down the hall, directly to the living room couch.

There I distracted myself from my debilitating lethargy as best I could with endless hours of inspirational TV and by comforting myself with videos of my loved ones. I sought out comedies to watch to encourage laughter to release my body's natural feel-good endorphins. Still, tears of pain fell from my eyes counting off the hours of the day until nightfall. Every system in my body felt raw and uncontrollable and my mind was bent on me taking notice.

My husband exhausted himself in caring for me, endlessly researching the possible cause of my symptoms and implementing anything he could think of to help me. Selfless in his attention, I could only pray that God would bless him in return as I watched him lose interest in so many things that he had always enjoyed. Traveling across the country, we sought help from medical and holistic experts alike. Devotedly, David administered my daily IV therapy, attending to my needs without complaint. We tried each treatment we found until it proved it would not be the answer and then we moved on to the next. Led by the arm and forced to eat, I seemed to become more of a living empty shell with each progressing day.

Praying through the insomnia, I lay as still as possible, unwilling to disturb my sleeping husband. I slowly turned my head to be met with the anguish in David's eyes as he kept a silent vigil watching over me in my torment. My tears fell afresh.

Detesting my weakness, I whispered, "I'm so sorry, David. You didn't sign up for this. I would understand if you moved on with your life."

"You don't know me if you think that I would, and you are wrong, I did sign up for this. It was written in our marriage vows. I wouldn't leave my comrades behind in Vietnam, and I will not leave you."

His words were a balm to my soul. David made sure that I heard them often. He knew that even his reassuring hand on my shoulder, meant to comfort me, could increase my pain. Daily the things that should have brought pleasure and meaning to life brought painful, nervous system sensory overload—happy laughter, the hum of a fan, the sun shining through the window, or even a light breeze. David made it his job to find ways encourage me and I welcomed each one.

> "Cast your burden on the Lord, and
> he will sustain you; He will never permit
> the righteous to be moved" (Ps. 55:22,
> ESV).

My case passed from one medical doctor to the next, yet we were no closer to a diagnosis than the day we first went to the emergency room. The illness progressed, and it became more certain that it was going to be up to us to figure out what was happening to me. In the meanwhile, I continued with rounds of castor oil packs, colonic therapy, and gall bladder cleanses that brought progressive relief to the unbearable pain and pressure in my digestive tract. As the days turned into weeks and I was unable to eat, my husband pressed our fruit, vegetable, and berry capsules into my hand at regular intervals throughout the day to keep me nourished.

Laser treatments reduced the crippling muscle pain. Intravenous vitamins and minerals minimized the weakness and diminished the uncontrollable jerking in my legs. Attempting to relieve the constant tilting, spinning, and nauseating debilitating dizziness, we incorporated essential oils, physical therapy, chiropractic, ozone therapy, and benign paroxysmal positional vertigo (BPPV) adjustments. We began the dance of one optimistic step forward and two steps seemingly backwards.

Every unexplainable symptom drove me deeper into the Sacred Heart of Jesus. I was seeking wisdom in an inexplicable situation. It became clear to me that it was easier to have hope and faith for someone else than it was to have it for myself. Every erroneous belief I held about suffering erupted, rising to the surface like an ugly pustule that I could not hide. What I thought (head knowledge) and what I believed (heart knowledge) began to separate like oil and water.

Every dark corner, every fear and doubt were illuminated by my suffering. I found myself with the opportunity to step out of agreement with any thought that held itself up against the Word of God and His promises. As I called more of Jesus into my heart, the cloying, disparaging, maligning weaknesses hiding there begged to be released, unable to share the space with His presence. In the dark of night, when insomnia and pain kept me from resting, one by one, I sat with my fears and asked God what it was that He wanted me to know.

> "Even though I walk through the darkest valley; I fear no evil; for you are with me; your rod and your staff; they comfort me" (Ps. 23:4, NIV).

One night the darkness around me briefly parted as I slipped from one level of sleeplessness to the next. Untangling the rosary that had wound tightly around my hand, I sensed a mystical presence in the room, a palpable love surrounding me, soothing my nerves, raising the hair in my skin. It was not spectacular like a sunset or a baby's smile or like the fact that our planet supports life or is held in its place in the universe. However, it was miraculous to me. In the twilight of sleep, as my prayers began to slip into the silence of forgetfulness, I was feeling a gentle yet firm tugging sensation deep inside my leg, not once but three distinct times. Now more awake than before, I lay still trying to assimilate what was happening.

I reasoned there were no small children in the house to wake me by nudging my leg, and I could hear my husband's rhythmic breathing as he slept beside me. Again, three distinct tugs felt deep inside my right leg. A feeling of relief began spreading as the three points of pain in my leg that I tried to ignore and that had caused me to limp for nearly three years. A third time I felt the gentle tugs and then I felt the pain float away into the darkness. "What was that?" I asked the Lord. "Insolence." The response came back to me so quickly that I turned my head to see if someone spoke. I had felt something leave me. The root of my wound that caused me to be constantly disappointed and dissatisfied and subconsciously made me feel like I needed to let everyone know it, had finally let go.

> "And he said to them, 'This kind cannot be driven out by anything but prayer'" (Mark 9:29, NASB).

I had been bewildered for years trying to understand why I could not seem to control my reaction to certain situations. In my healing prayer, with the help of those who prayed with me, I had begun to peel back the layers of protection that I built up around myself while trying to grow up. I had infinite patience with babies in my care but had selective forgiveness and understanding for people who (as I know now) reflected to me my own shortcomings.

After I came to know Jesus more intimately, I tried to control this intolerant part of me with sheer numbers of Hail Mary's, which often left me exhausted and feeling worse about myself the next time I slipped. However, the time spent on each one of those rosary beads led me to this moment. Surrendering the weakness and pain in my leg, *God's mercy and grace* met me to answer to my prayer and I was healed. In that moment of elation, I felt as though I should never want for anything ever again. I had been given a glimpse of the power of God.

Unfortunately, my euphoria lasted only until I encountered the first person who inadvertently interrupted me or attempted to change my plans. However, even as I drew in a breath to raise my voice with a programmed characteristically sharp reply, I became very aware that I now needed to take responsibility for my reaction. It brought back to my mind the gratitude that I felt when I became free of my leg pain that night and I caught myself gentling my response. Victory! I was beginning to recognize the gift of grace more readily and I allowed it to help me respond kindly, one encounter at a time.

> "Do not be conformed to this world, but *be transformed by the renewing of your mind*, so that you may prove what the will of God is, that which is good and acceptable and perfect" (Rom. 12:2, NASB; emphasis added).

My life was a training ground, and I was discovering how God was equipping me. Symptoms receded and resurfaced with no rhyme or reason. I pursued answers relentlessly: x-rays, physical therapy, massage, nutrition, and emotional healing. While contemplating what my body was trying to tell me, I was led to a deeper understanding of the origins of pain I had experienced in my life. Some of which I had brought upon myself through immaturity or mistakes, some I felt were inflicted because of others. When I came to a place where I could no longer find my way out of the maze of pain, I decided to simply lie down and wait for God to come and rescue me.

How many prayers had brought me to this moment? I knew it was time to face what I had feared the most— fear itself. For years, fears had permeated my thoughts and influenced my actions, but I had failed to recognize the reason for its invasion. After years of nightmares where it expressed itself in a million graphic ways, this night it came to me like a gentle tap on my shoulder and I opened my eyes to find it staring at me in the face. It seemed almost innocent, like an old friend asking if I recognized her and not the monster I had imagined seeping out of the small box that I had sealed and buried in a tomb of despair when my son was ill. I now welcomed the encounter with my fears.

I had come face-to-face with the part of me that was afraid. It was the part that I had dragged through the years of my son's illness, begging to be noticed, while it kicked and screamed like a thrashing toddler. My fear would wait until it seemed everything was going well then show up at my door unannounced, again making demands for my attention. However, I had always found a way to silence it.

All but forgotten, the fear was now causing me physical pain as it rose to the surface because my body could no longer contain it. There was a part of me that had formed the habit of presuming the worse and it was unable to rationalize whether I had real cause to be afraid. I learned in my healing journey that the part of me that was afraid *was* a very real part of me. I felt I had valid reasons to feel fearful and act out of fear because of the painful experiences in my past that supported those beliefs. Now that God was illuminating me with His Truth, it was no longer true that I needed to be afraid. The fear needed to go.

> "The Lord is my light and my salvation—whom shall I fear? The Lord is the stronghold of my life—of whom shall I be afraid?" (Ps. 27:1, NIV).

When inviting Jesus into the places where I first developed the belief that I had good reason to be afraid, I began to understand why I resisted in letting go of fear. I had places of mistakes, disappointment, and miscommunication that needed God's touch. In my prayer, I held tight to the rope that connected memory to memory, even when the cord slowly unraveled to no more than a thread, however, I always reached my destination of healing before it disintegrated in my hand. The Lord always showed up in time to *shine His light and truth* on my beliefs. Not dependent on or constrained by time (Heb. 13:8), Jesus saved me, is saving me, and continues to save me still.

> "And He said to me, 'My grace is sufficient for you, for My strength is made perfect in weakness.' Therefore, most gladly I will rather boast in my infirmities, that the power of Christ may rest upon me" (2 Cor. 12:9, NIV).

Countless times a day I reminded myself of the pledge I had made to God when we were fighting for my son's life: "Though He slay me, yet will I trust Him" (Job 13:15). By sheer will, I forced myself to "rise up" each day. Continuously praising God made that possible. Soon, I was waking up to the same song of praise still echoing in my mind that I had fallen asleep to, as if the angels had taken over the chorus through the night.

It became frightfully disturbing when my misery began to feel like a new normal to me. All the MRIs and CAT scans I had, which held their own risks, and blood tests of every kind left me no closer to finding what was wrong with me. Until, upon hearing of my symptoms, my husband's friend gave him a book called *Insights into Lyme Disease Treatment: 13 Lyme-Literate Health Care Practitioners Share Their Healing Strategies*. The book clearly listed each of my symptoms. Unbelievably, none of the medical doctors I consulted even suggested my symptoms could be from Lyme disease! I soon discovered the simple reason. The mainstream Infectious Diseases Society of America insists there is no such thing as chronic Lyme disease. Medical insurance companies fail to acknowledge the need for treatment deeming it as "experimental, unproven, and unwarranted." Medical doctors who use unconventional treatments for Lyme disease risk punishment by medical boards. I was left without medical resources since I had not experienced a recent tick bite. I also learned that standard testing could rarely confirm Lyme disease.

When I opened the book to a chapter by Dr. Lee Cowden, I felt as if the missing pieces to a puzzle I had been struggling to finish had just fallen from the sky. Dr. Cowden was the doctor who first spoke to me at the wellness center in Texas where I had taken Ethan in our attempt to save his life. His comforting words to me back then now echoed, "You are in the right place."

I was confronted with my ignorance once again. I thought Lyme disease was just a rash easily cured with a round of antibiotics. I was dismayed to discover that Lyme disease is caused not by the tick bite itself but by a spirochete bacterium (*Borrelia burgdorferi*). Transmitted not only by deer ticks but also by mosquitoes, brown recluse spiders, flies, ants, birds, mice, blood transfusions, and bodily fluids during unprotected sex. The bacterium can transform into different forms to avoid being identified by the immune system and antibiotics. Boring through bone, muscle, and brain, it takes nothing short of a private detective to track it. As we were painfully aware, it can leave behind a plethora of destruction. We were left baffled, overwhelmed by my debilitating symptoms, our finances exhausted.

I learned that there is a myriad of coinfections that complicate the treatment process and must be dealt with in specific cycles. This demands a team of Lyme-literate health professionals to help the patient cope and heal. Over three hundred thousand new cases are diagnosed each year according to the Center for Disease Control, yet standard blood testing for Lyme has proven to be insufficient and inaccurate more often than not.

It is estimated that for as many as are diagnosed with Lyme, there may be just as many that have been misdiagnosed or are suffering with no diagnosis or treatment. Lyme-literate doctors find that the symptoms of over three hundred conditions can be attributed to Lyme. Crohn's disease, chronic fatigue syndrome, ALS, MS, Alzheimer's, colitis, encephalitis, fibromyalgia, fifth disease, arthritis, cystitis, IBS, lupus, prostatitis, psychiatric disorders (bipolar, depression), Sjogren's syndrome, sleep disorders, thyroid disease, and many more.

When it was recommended to me that I watch the documentary *Under Our Skin*, I realized that I was not alone in my nightmare. There were thousands suffering without diagnosis or any real help. Similar to my case, others were being passed from specialist to specialist as undiagnosed Lyme and its coinfections presented unexplainable symptoms.

Piecing together the timeline of when the symptoms began, we realized it was shortly after a hip injury during a Pilate's exercise class. The torn gluteus medius muscle at the insertion site had not healed, even after ten months of various physical therapies. I had rejected the idea of the proposed aggressive, invasive surgery since strict food elimination to reduce the inflammation had made it bearable. Although, soon after that injury, I began having pain throughout my entire body and a host of other unexplainable symptoms. I now read that flare-ups of chronic Lyme disease often happen after an injury or other trauma. In effect, it becomes the straw that breaks the camel's back no matter how healthy the person may appear.

The immune system becomes completely overwhelmed. The spirochetes and coinfections invade joints, tissues, heart, liver, lungs, spleen, and optic nerve. It crosses the blood brain barrier and causes neurological dysfunction.

Everything from the soles of the feet to the roots of hair can be affected. Bright light, noise, and touch become intolerable with complete sensory overload. No part, including emotions, is left unaffected.

At this point, even my loving family had a difficult time understanding how incapacitated I had become. I could not allow this new information to negate the trust I had in God. I regularly called to mind the years of Ethan's journey to wellness and recommitted to incorporating all the healing principles we knew of for myself. It played like an old movie, just new actors.

Most days I could not form two words that did not scream out of the depths of my self-absorption. To cope, I replaced doubts of ever becoming well with the praise of God's Holy Name. Loud enough for my soul to hear it, I prayed to be healed, *"Father Forever, God Hero, Prince of Peace, Emanuel, My Shepherd and Healer, My Teacher and Provider, I see it as done!"* I recounted over and over to myself the wonderful deeds He had done throughout history, in the world and in my own life. I would not cease until I talked my spirit back into humble obedience to the Word, committing to surrender even in the suffering.

> "Why, my soul, are you downcast?
> Why so disturbed within me? Put your
> hope in God, for I will yet praise him, my
> Savior and my God" (Ps. 43:5, NIV).

My husband and I wasted no time in calling Dr. Lee Cowden remembering how he had helped my son so many years before. Once again traveling to Texas to see Dr. Cowden, we began the laborious work of untying the many knots of illness. Led by the arm into the waiting room, I sank onto the sofa praying for strength to be able to rise. The testing there revealed the presence of babesia, bartonella, and borrelia. It was what we expected. I now needed to apply to myself the healing modalities of eliminating the infection, detoxification, and providing organ support, just as I had when my son was ill. The testing also revealed how toxic I was, even detecting a host of chemotherapy drugs. At my questioning, the doctor explained that through skin-to-skin contact, through my son's sweat and tears and the handling of his toxic medication, I too had absorbed the chemotherapy drugs from my son's treatment and they were still lingering.

After taking a detailed family health history, Dr. Cowden spent time explaining that the most concerning problem my case presented was my struggling lymph system. Referred to as being a non-eliminator, he stressed the importance of opening and supporting the eliminatory organs: skin, lymph, colon, kidneys, and lungs. I was instructed in the invaluable importance of skin brushing and using an infrared sauna. Asking what I understood about generational healing, he stressed I should continue to address emotional and spiritual healing as well.

Once back at the hotel room, I lined up the remedies on the nightstand and stared at the carefully detailed instructions. It was not long before the inner battle began. How could this be happening to me? Why? Why would I wind up in this situation? Had I not learned enough? Surrendered enough? Trusted enough? I was able to see the spiritual battle when I was fighting for my son's life. All I could see now— was me. Then I suddenly recognized it—the enemy's tactic to lure me away from the source of my peace.

> "Therefore put on the full armor of God, so that when the day of evil comes, you may be able to stand your ground, and after you have done everything, to stand" (Eph. 6:13, NIV).

I knew whatever was to come, I needed to trust, even more. Wherever I was, God was with me. This was my situation; it was happening, so God was allowing it for a purpose. Standing beside the pool of His Divine Will, I looked forlornly into its depths. Where else could I go? I was trapped in a body that would not work right. I could not make it work right in a moment. However, He could. I even believed deep in my heart that He would. I focused on what I wanted most. Yes, I wanted to be well. I wanted to stop being a burden and stop spending such an enormous amount of money on this condition. I wanted control over my body. I wanted peace. I wanted to rest and be released from the pain.

Then I realized what I wanted most was to hear my Savior's voice, to be held closely by His love. I yearned to be near Him—at His birth, as He played, as He grew, as He taught, as He healed, as He suffered, as He died, as He rose again. I grasped my rosary and with it, reciting the Holy Mysteries, visually following Jesus through each stage of His life, from His conception to the coming of His Holy Spirit, I was with Him. In those thoughts and with that longing, I found peace in what mattered most.

Surrendering, I slowly lay down on my side fixing my gaze on a nearby object, in a feeble attempt to stop feeling like the room was tilting. The effort of moving forced a moan to pass my lips. Closing my eyes, I pushed the beads of the rosary over my fingers, calling on the Mother of God to pray with me. "Hail Mary, full of grace, the Lord is with thee. Blessed are you among women and blessed is the fruit of thy womb . . . Jesus . . . Jesus . . . Jesus . . ."

Every pain in my body, first searing, then crushing, then throbbing, then piercing, I drew into the bead and into the Holy Name. My eyes fixed upon Jesus. No plea. No explanation. No reasoning. No expectation. My breath became a prayer as my mind surrendered, embraced, and numbed to the pain. Peace came. More than willing that this night be my last, yet welcoming whatever God deemed best for me, without preference for life or death, I drew in a deep breath. I felt myself sinking into a blessed silent space and I yearned for it. With forbearance, I prayed, "Holy Mary, Mother of God, pray for us sinners, now and at the hour of our death. Amen."

"In peace I will both lie down and sleep, For You alone, O Lord, make me dwell in safety" (Ps. 4:8, ESV).

It is hard to describe pain that does not end. Each day can become a cycle of misery and hopelessness if our mind accepts that that is all there is to it. If eradicating the pain and seeking relief is the only goal, then it is easy to despair when that does not happen. Even the Only One without sin suffered greatly. Grace abounds not only when we imitate Jesus's example of suffering with love and surrendering to God's will as He did but also when immersed in meditating on His passion.

Saint Rose of Lima said, "We would not complain about our cross or troubles if we knew the scales that weigh the afflictions distributed to us. Hidden in each are immeasurable joys." In the same way, Saint Vincent de Paul encourages us, "If we only knew the precious treasure hidden in infirmities, we would receive them with the same joy with which we receive the greatest benefits and would bear them without ever complaining or showing signs of weariness."

If that is the way of our Savior, there is promise for those who follow. The saints strove to live that truth in their own suffering while earnestly working to alleviate the suffering of others. When all has been done for the moment and there is nothing else we can do, still there is a way to find peace. We can allow ourselves to rest in God's presence until the next thing we can do arises.

> "When you go through deep waters
> and great trouble, I will be with you.
> When you go through rivers of difficulty,
> you will not drown!" (Isa. 43:2, NLV).

As the rapid detox from Lyme and its coinfections progressed, we were compelled to consult a naturopath closer to home to monitor the process and implement the support protocol. I learned that Dr. Joseph Cataldo from Elkhart, Indiana, had eradicated his own chronic Lyme as well as his wife's and many others. Both attributed their success to using the TrueRife frequency device based on the research of Dr. Raymond Rife (www.truerife.com) while at the same time building up the body's immune system.

For quite a while, it felt as though every step forward just took me further from the end. I reminded myself it takes diligence and patience to overcome *dis*-ease (the absence of ease). More often than not, it looked like we followed a crooked path with many detours rather than a straight road. I took comfort knowing that we were solidly committed to following Dr. Cataldo's recommendations to the letter. Giving up was not an option.

> "Every valley shall be filled in, every mountain and hill made low. The crooked roads shall become straight, the rough ways smooth" (Luke 3:5, NIV).

The route we had chosen to take required a huge investment emotionally, physically, and financially. Aware of my blessings, I thanked God that I had such a wonderful husband and family to take care of me. I knew that not everyone with this disease did. I prayed fervently for all those who were suffering. I prayed for the "impoverished fully insured" who did not have a bank account to empty or a house to sell like we did, to pay for the necessary treatments not covered by medical insurance. I prayed relentlessly that God would move in power to stop the double bind people found themselves in and somehow stop the spread of the Lyme disease epidemic.

Having the ability to burrow into cells and tendons and to change its appearance, the Borelli is not easily eradicated and leaves a wide array of destruction in its wake. Homeopathy is not a quick fix, but it is thorough. Instead of suppressing symptoms, we were supporting my body's efforts to regain homeostasis and aiding its ability to heal. I learned how cannabidiol oil (CBD) assisted in that process and how it greatly relieved neurological disorders, pain, and anxiety, and I began to benefit immensely from using it (more information and ordering at http://www.hemp worx.com/ealbrecht). Detoxification needed to be done gently while supporting each detoxification pathway and that would take time. Learning and processing this new information would take time.

To fill that time, I continued my quest to rest in God. My heart searched for answers. If God didn't use such circumstances to stretch me, would I grow at all? Would the lessons be repeated until I learned them? Was it not better to be well, better to be a caretaker than to be the one needing care? I was capable and adept. When that was taken away, what was left of me? While I was caring for Ethan during his illness, I was able to surrender everything for my son's sake. Now, unable to function on my own, I was completely dependent on others and utterly miserable burdening them with my care. God showed me that both sides of that coin, caring for others as well as being cared for, were equally valuable and important to Him.

God alone could bring not only good but also redemptive gifts from everything I was experiencing. He revealed His presence, even in the years that I was not consciously aware of God, when revisiting the memories in my healing prayer. Nothing is beyond God's faithful love—not an unplanned pregnancy, an accident, a mistake, an unjust harm, an illness, the pain of a difficult relationship, or a heartbreaking loss. Hour to hour, day to day, I was dependent on God's grace to keep and direct me. He would not miss any opportunity to help me grow in His strength by using the very things that made me weak. I began to surrender all the wildness in my heart that had resisted His will or anything in me that objected to remaining in His peace.

Daily I yearned to hear God's voice and to learn all He wanted me to know. I began with rosary in hand, vividly bringing the life of Jesus to my mind. Praying the Holy Mysteries of the Rosary on my beads, I could recall Him leaving His heavenly throne to become flesh, to be born in a lowly manger and to walk the earth doing the will of His Father. Each decade of the rosary called to mind His ministry, His miracles, and the fulfillment of His Father's promise.

I slowly said each Hail Mary prayer, repeating the words of the Angel Gabriel, "Hail, full of grace, the Lord is with you" (Luke 1:28), and of Elizabeth, the mother of John the Baptist, when greeting the Blessed Mother, "Blessed are you among women," (Luke 1:42a) and "Blessed is the fruit of thy womb" (Luke 1:42b), and with each repetition I acknowledged and revered God's plan to give His Son to redeem the world and the Virgin Mary's fiat which made it reality.

I wanted to cooperate with God's ongoing work in my life. In earnest I prayed, "What should I do? How will I know?" In my silence, I sensed our loving Blessed Mother reminding me by her example, "Trust Him. You will not miss it. Be at peace and joyfully wait." The altar I built with my prayer was piled high with the most infinitesimal to the greatest offerings that I had, the things I considered accomplishments to those things I simply had found pleasure in doing before and could now no longer do. The ability to walk a straight line, turn my head, speak a full sentence, lie down to sleep, drive a car, or eat a meal—it was all beyond my control and I endeavored to let it all go.

> "He said unto me, My grace is sufficient for thee; for My strength is made perfect in weakness. Most gladly therefore will I rather glory in my infirmities that the power of Christ may rest upon me" (2 Cor. 12:9, KJV).

I soon began to see steady and considerable improvement when traveling to the Bremen Clinic, in Bremen, Georgia, for the support IV therapy that was recommended by Dr. Cataldo. I sat in the quiet morning hours there, my bible on my lap. I glanced at the words I had highlighted sitting by my son's side years ago while sequestered in his bone marrow transplant hospital room. My fingers again passed over the words of faith I read: "As for me, I trust in your merciful love. Let my heart rejoice in your saving help!" (Ps. 13:5). I caressed the verse gently, absorbing its strength through my skin like a sponge. Soaking up each word, I turned it over and over in my mind until it found the same rhythm as the beat of my heart. The Living Word coursed through my body and with little effort pulled me to my feet to face another day.

> "Praise the Lord, my soul; all my inmost being, praise His holy name. Praise the Lord, my soul and forget not all his benefits, who forgives all your sins and heals all your diseases" (Ps. 103:1–3, NIV).

Five years passed by since the day I fell ill with Lyme disease, and my unexplainable, debilitating symptoms had sent me running to the emergency room. Three years since an accurate diagnosis and any helpful treatment began. A year had passed since the debilitating vertigo finally stopped and six months since I became fully functioning, able to go for a walk and drive a car again. I now looked out over the blue water of the Florida Intracoastal Waterway, contemplating God's goodness and mercy.

My husband and I were spending a healing winter away from the cold and snow of the North. The balmy spring breeze rustling the palms drew my attention, and I noticed a single dolphin's fin periodically appearing as it made its way up the channel. I wondered at the solitary dolphin and how it came to be traveling alone. Soon there appeared another, then another. Even though I did not at first see the others, they obviously had been there the whole time. They were fellow travelers on the same journey, having the same experience but on another level.

It occurred to me that I was not alone in my journey, the Trinity—Father, Son, and the Holy Spirit—though invisible, accompanied me all along the way. There were many times when I could sense their presence and times when others told me they could clearly see God at work, even when I could not.

> "Let us hold unswervingly to the hope we profess, for He who promised is faithful. And let us consider how we may spur one another on toward love and good deeds, not giving up meeting together, as some are in the habit of doing, but encouraging one another—and all the more as you see the Day approaching." (Heb. 10:23–25, NIV)

We may find a struggle of faith when faced with illness, loss, and death. However painful, it is worth enduring. Naturally, when those we love are suffering, we want to help in every way that we can. Our Heavenly Father is no different. What *can we* do when there is nothing *we can* do? We can still affect those things that are beyond our control with prayer. To sing a song of praise to God carries twice the power. In times of trial, our song proclaims our trust to all who hear, including ourselves.

"Praise the Lord, O my soul, and forget not all His benefits—who forgives all your sins and heals all your diseases, who redeems your life from the pit and crowns you with love and compassion" (Ps. 103:3–4, NIV).

Disease is becoming more and more complicated from the effects of our world's toxicity. The body's inability to handle the process of detoxification and repair can drive us to despair and we may begin to lose hope. We need to remember that the body is programmed by God for healing. It will always be drawn in that direction. When using God's food—whole food—as our fuel, the body will rebuild and repair. Accepting a diagnosis without working to correct the imbalance in the body that caused the illness or disease is an exercise in foolishness. Prescription medication is at best a Band-Aid and can often be a hindrance. For me, my prayer led me to find health professionals that embraced integrative, functional medicine and who understood the body's many needs in a health crisis.

In recent years, there has been a surge of unrest from those of us who have become disillusioned with drug-related solutions offered by a pharmaceutically trained medical community. It is imperative that our voices be heard as we witness a system that rewards the efforts of lobbyists for multimillion-dollar pharmaceutical and chemical companies, one that leaves a sick, toxic society to bear the burden for carelessness.

Many other countries are protecting their citizens from GMOs, aerial spraying and application of pesticides, and harmful chemical food and body products. Yet, in the United States, we and our children are often still being used as guinea pigs in a treacherous science experiment. In our country, we have become much like pawns in a game of global food domination for financial gain. If there were ever a time that people needed hope, it is now. This is not a time to underestimate the power of prayer. We need to believe that God is leading us to our healing. To do that, we need to become sensitive to His prompting in our hearts where He speaks.

> "But if any of you lacks wisdom, let him ask of God, who gives to all gener-ously and without reproach, and it will be given to him" (James 1:5, ESV).

The day my son was diagnosed with cancer I believed that God *could* heal him. I also believed (again and again) that He *would* heal him. I have no doubt in my mind that He did heal him. Yet I needed to learn to stop allowing the things that would cause and contribute to Ethan's illness and begin to do the things that would keep him well. I was being made into someone willing to be pliable in God's hands, not letting the way I wanted things to be done inter-fere with what God wanted to do. God taught me to pray so I would remain close enough to follow Him.

Faith, the hope of things unseen, and obedience moves the heart of God. When the apostles asked why they did not see results when they prayed, Jesus answered them by saying, "Because of the littleness of your faith; for truly I say to you, if you have faith as small as a mustard seed, you can say to this mountain, 'Move from here to there,' and it will move. Nothing will be impossible for you" (Matt. 17:20). Jesus felt the power go out of Him when touched by the woman with the hemorrhage. It is written, "And He said to her, 'Daughter, your faith has made you well; go in peace'" (Luke 8:48).

> "But the wisdom that comes from heaven is first of all pure; then peace-loving, considerate, submissive, full of mercy and good fruit, impartial and sincere" (James 3:17).

We are living in a world that is reaping the consequences of disregarding the presence and plan of the Creator. I prayed for wisdom and I was given a glimpse of God's perspective. In many ways, we have lost much of the wisdom that for generations was shared on the front porches and at the dinner tables of homes across the country. The wisdom gained in a life of connection and sensible contemplation seems to have been replaced with entertainment, distraction, and the mentality of a driven and disposable society.

Although God's truth had been spelled out in Holy Scripture all along, it was only with the help of the Holy Spirit that I could read it with understanding. The Holy Spirit enables us to accomplish all that God commanded and Jesus taught, and He will never fail to come when we call on Him for help. He will inspire us when to *wait on the Lord* and when to *step out in faith*. He is never late, even should our choices take us in what seems to be the wrong direction, or in the least, a very long detour.

> "But seek ye first the kingdom of God,
> and His righteousness; and all these things
> shall be added unto you" (Matt. 6:33,
> ESV).

I was filled with nostalgia as I pulled open the massive oak door to Saint Patrick's Catholic Church while visiting my hometown. The ease with which it opened was in heavy contrast to the memory of how I struggled to move it as a child. Walking into that church never failed to arouse my childhood memory of the funeral Mass for my oldest brother Nick. My sister's college folk group sang Pete Seeger's "Turn! Turn! Turn!" from the book of Ecclesiastes 3:1–9 and it was forever imprinted in my heart. "To everything—turn, turn, turn. There is a season—turn, turn, turn. And a time to every purpose under heaven." Fleetingly, the melody crossed my lips as I walked up the side aisle of the church. I had been asked by a friend to assist in the music that night. Halting midway to the altar, I dropped my guitar to the toe of my boot. "Oh no, you've got to be kidding me!" I thought. From where I stood, I could see and recognized Sister James Marion, my high school geometry teacher. Decades had passed since I last saw her but the memory of the trouble I caused her in class was crystal-clear.

When I saw the guitar in her hand, I lifted my eyes to heaven and began to laugh. I realized we would be playing music together that night for the parish healing mass. Hesitantly, I approached. Doing my best to swallow the slice of humble pie I had just been handed, I wondered how I should proceed. I had caused her more than my share of the gray hairs on her holy head by repeatedly skipping her class and refusing to do the assigned class work. God bless her, I sincerely prayed.

"Hello, sister, do you remember me?" I asked, introducing myself. "Looks like I'll be joining you tonight." She looked intently at me for a moment until I sheepishly added, "I'd like to say right off, before we start, how sorry I am that I gave you so much trouble in high school." Slowly a smile of recognition spread across her face and taking my hand, she said, "All is forgiven. All that is important is that you are here now!"

I have had many kinds of healing along my journey, some subtle, some not. Sometimes I am actively seeking it and sometimes it arrives in the most surprising ways. We are promised that wisdom will be given liberally and ungrudgingly to all who ask. I encourage you to ask! Healing is promised because of our faith. Have faith! Faith grows by thinking God's thoughts instead of and despite our own. Take every thought captive and speak aloud the Word of God! Jesus *is* the reward for those who do. Everything He has taught me, everything that I have often struggled to learn, has become part of me and part of my story and it is a good one.

"My people, hear my teaching; listen to the words of my mouth. I will open my mouth with a parable; I will utter hidden things, things from of old—things we have heard and known, things our ancestors have told us. We will not hide them from their descendants; we will tell the next generation the praiseworthy deeds of the LORD, his power, and the wonders he has done." (Ps. 78:1–4, NIV)

The road to health was not an easy one to follow, but the process was simplified when God led us to the solution that complemented our juicing program so well. Now we were even growing our own produce on our patio in the city and it was liberating. Three tall vertical Juice Plus+® Tower Gardens stood right outside my kitchen window. The hydroponic growing systems were growing our own organic greens, and they thrived in abundance just steps from my table, assuring me that the produce we are eating is just moments from the vine.

Stepping outside, I pick a ripe cucumber and a half dozen celery stalks from the Tower Garden, adding them to a pile of freshly picked kale in my colander. I sigh in contentment as I walk a few steps across the patio and reenter the kitchen. Tossing the produce into the blender, I add chilled coconut water, turmeric, ginger, and lemon to make our morning green drink. I marvel at how our life has changed. Living food has been reestablished in its proper place, high on my family's list of priorities and there will be no turning back.

I believe that God delivered the answer to my desperate prayer for help right into the hands of the man I would come to love, that night I prayed so earnestly when my son lay close to death. Before I knew my husband, God's hand had directed David off the beaten path, to a juice bar inside a health food store, in a small town in Florida. There he struck up a conversation about the benefits of whole food and organic vegetables with the owner, naturopath Dr. Jan Young.

Jan was quick to see the convenience and validity of the Juice Plus+° encapsulated fruits and vegetables that David shared with her and she signed onto his team. She wasted no time in sharing it with her own family and those she cared about. Eventually, she in turn brought the Tower Gardens that she used to grow her own organic produce to the Juice Plus+° Company. The company took on the distribution of the Tower Gardens and finally making its way to me, the circle was complete. Living nourishment, God's food, was now literally within my reach.

> "But I have raised you up for this very
> purpose, that I might show you My power
> and that my Name might be proclaimed
> in all the earth" (Exod. 9:16, NIV).

Since consuming fruit, vegetables, and berries in capsules every day, we now crave and happily eat those foods that give us life and health. We have become more aware of the deception that surrounds the current mainstream food supply and now have the confidence to more easily sidestep the companies and restaurants that promote the consumption of toxic and carcinogenic ingredients. We know that eating those things will surely make us sick. Our knowledge drives us to daily seek out real, organic, fresh whole food for our family. It is also a tremendous help that we surround ourselves with like-minded believers who will encourage and support our efforts.

Each morning I am invigorated as I deeply inhale the scents of lemon, ginger, and greens that waft from the blender while making our daily green drink. As Ethan passes through the kitchen on his way out the door, I press a glass into his hand. He has heard it before and he'll hear it again. "You know, don't you, that if it weren't for Juice Plus+°, I would be following you to college next year with this green drink in my hand!" I wink and then laugh as he rolls his eyes. "Yes, I know," he sighs seriously. Hugging Ethan tightly, I feel excitement knowing he is stepping out into the world healthier for my efforts and truly understanding the need to continue to make his health a priority.

> "In returning [to Me] and rest you
> shall be saved, in quietness and confident
> trust is your strength" (Isa. 30:15, KJV).

Is deepening our faith by learning and speaking the Scriptures an assurance that our sick children will be healed? Is learning to protect our family by reading labels, detoxifying our bodies, avoiding toxins and eating organically a guarantee that we and our loved ones will not develop cancer? Unfortunately, there are no guarantees but there are plenty of God's promises to hold on to. We live in a corrupt, toxic, and imperfect world. However, there is *much* that we can do to reduce our risk of disease. There is *much* we can do to aid our body's healing abilities. There is *much* we can do to increase our peace by drawing close to God, holding fast to His promise that He will never abandon us in our difficulties, whatever they may be.

> "I have told you these things, so that in me you may have peace. In this world you will have trouble. But take heart! I have overcome the world" (John 16:33, NIV).

I was not looking for God but for relief from my pain long ago, on the day of my unintended confession. I cannot fully fathom the depth of the gift that was masquerading as trouble in my life. Acknowledging my wretchedness released a beauty I never realized I possessed. I have been taught that nothing will be wasted. When we fall in life, we are promised the strength to rise. It is never too late to begin or to begin again. There is nothing too big for God to handle—not our darkest secrets, our biggest problems, our deepest hurts, or our greatest loss.

> "After you have suffered a little while, the God of all grace, who has called you this eternal glory in Christ, will himself

restore, confirm, strengthen, and establish
you" (1 Pet. 5:10, ESV).

The debilitating pain I suffered with Lyme disease became a weapon of warfare for the kingdom when it drew me nearer to God. Pain is no longer useful to the enemy to torment me when it becomes a call to prayer. Saint Augustine wrote, "Let us understand that God is a physician, and that suffering is a medicine for salvation, not a punishment for damnation." I found that I can turn the table on the enemy's schemes to invoke fear and doubt by recognizing it as a call to praise God who heals, protects, and guides.

"Ask and it will be given to you; seek
and you will find; knock and the door will
be opened to you" (Matt. 7:7, NIV).

If we do not believe our prayers will be answered, we will most likely see proof that we are right. We can expect the enemy to happily feed any unbelief and reinforce it as well. If we *do* believe what we ask will be given, we will need to be prepared to fight for our belief because the enemy will most certainly do his best to wrestle our hope and God's promise away from us. Decide to believe. Hold tenaciously to your ground trusting God will not disappoint you. If it still does not appear that things are working out as we would like, *Trust Even More* that God has another plan and will never abandon us in our need.

"But when you ask, you must believe and not doubt, because the one who doubts is like a wave of the sea, blown and tossed by the wind" (James 1:6, NIV).

Being exposed to a rich faith-filled upbringing was a blessing that undoubtedly helped me find my way back to God when I became lost. There is a Gospel message written in each of our lives no matter what our circumstance. There is a treasure in our story. One blessing that I received from being surrounded with so many brothers and sisters growing up is knowing that there is *always* room for one more. This attitude has been a great source of joy in my life, from making many friends in school to welcoming each of my own children with joy despite the hardship I was experiencing to caring for other's children in my daycare, to reaching out to build a team-based business. It can be difficult to look forward to life with enthusiasm, enjoying the path we are on, when we are unsure where it will take us. It is made easier by trusting that in every circumstance we encounter, God is equipping us for something good. Our determination to see it through to the finish will be rewarded. In Jesus's Name, we have authority to pray in confidence and expect results.

"I have fought a good fight, I have finished my course, I have kept the faith: Henceforth there is laid up for me a crown of righteousness, which the Lord, the righteous judge, shall give me at that day: and not to me only, but unto all them also that have longed for his appearance" (2 Tim. 4:7–8, KJV).

I learned that once my fears were placed in the hands of the Great Physician, healing would occur. At times FEAR (False Evidence Appearing Real) stands like a mountain before us, and it takes the antidote of FEAR (*f*aith *e*xpecting *a*mazing *r*esults) to remedy it. The factors of my son's illness, the ramifications of human error, were corrected when using the remedies that God created. Interestingly, the homeopathy we used is a system for treating illness that uses very minute amounts of natural substances to initiate a healing response in the ill person, that if given to a healthy person would produce symptoms of disease. God often uses nature to teach us valuable lessons. God provided Moses with the remedy His people needed using the likeness of what was meant for their harm.

> "Then the Lord said to Moses, 'Make a fiery serpent, and set it on a pole; and it shall be that everyone who is bitten, when he looks at it, shall live.' So Moses made a bronze serpent, and put it on a pole; and so it was, if a serpent had bitten anyone, when he looked at the bronze serpent, he lived." (Num. 21:4–9, ESV)

Through the TPM healing process, I recognized that I had created patterns of behavior to avoid uncomfortable feelings, even when my avoidance solution was no less painful. Every emotion buried alive attributed to how long it would take to heal. However, once I was freed from the emotional pain I was carrying, my body began to heal rapidly. It is through prayer, God's Word, and His work in me, that accomplishes my ongoing transformation.

Processing my strong emotions through healing prayer made the inner change evident. I began to recognize that I am now able to stop eating before becoming too full, no longer waiting until my stomach hurts to signal I have had enough. I notice I am better able to discern relationships and situations, which results in making better decisions. When faced with confrontation, I feel free to choose my actions, no longer ruled by a knee-jerk reaction.

> "Then shall your light break forth like the dawn, and your healing shall spring up speedily; your righteousness shall go before you; the glory of the Lord shall be your rear guard" (Isa. 58:8, ESV).

When things happen in our lives that we have no control over, we can be assured that God is still at work. Pursuing Him above all things will not leave us disappointed. Doubt and confusion can steal our peace when bad things happen if we only have an intellectual understanding of God's love for us. However, the results of having a personal experience of Jesus's love and healing cannot be easily taken away from us. Do not forget that we have an enemy who would keep us from our help and our purpose. When God has given us so much proof that prayer works, why would we not all fall to our knees and ask Him for all that we need? God wants to do something extraordinary and looks for someone who will believe for it.

> "For the eyes of the LORD roam throughout the entire earth, to strengthen those whose heart is true to him" (2 Chron. 16:9a, NIV).

As long as the enemy can keep us upset and frustrated, he can prevent us from hearing and seeing God's plan. When we surrender our heart to Jesus, He will instill in us the gifts of the Holy Spirit to defeat the enemy's tactics. How delighted we are as parents to see any honorable characteristic displayed in our children, just as Our Heavenly Father desires to see the holiness of His Son reflected in us.

> "And we all, who with unveiled faces contemplate the Lord's glory, are being transformed into His image with ever-increasing glory, which comes from the Lord, who is the Spirit" (2 Cor. 3:18, NIV).

God promises He will be with us through it all. He knows every word of our story and accepts us with love, compassion, understanding, and mercy. That is who He is. He is especially close to us in our pain, our loss, our grief, and disappointment. When our eyes are opened to

His presence in our suffering, we will recognize Him. He desires to comfort us, to relieve us, and to heal us. Saint Peter Chrysologus, Doctor of the Church, explains; God knew He would be believed by restoring His creation. "God knew that it was more glorious to forgive than to punish, to repair what was ruined rather than to preserve what was made."

> "Just as Moses lifted up the snake in the wilderness, so the Son of Man must be lifted up, that everyone who believes may have eternal life in him. For God so loved the world that he gave his one and only Son, that whoever believes in him shall not perish but have eternal life. For God did not send his Son into the world to condemn the world, but to save the world through him." (John 3:14–16, NIV)

God by His nature is Love, it is who He is. When we patiently trust Him to act on our behalf, He can bring sweetness to our acceptance and peace among the stormy unrest around us. It is always God's plan for us to remain united with Him. The earth and heavenly realm are divided by such a thin veil when we have God's Holy Spirit living and working within us. *We can* ask for more of God. He will reveal His presence to us, making us more aware that we are not alone. His desire for intimacy draws us to His table.

"When He had reclined at the table with them, He took the bread and blessed it, and breaking it, He began giving it to them. Then their eyes were opened and they recognized Him" (Luke 24:30–31, NASB).

We are creatures who long for communion with their Creator. The Blessed Sacrament, the humble hiding place masking God's power from the proud, confounds the world. Yet we are united to the Father in that very special way when we receive His Beloved Son in the Eucharist in the Holy Sacrament of the Mass. It is a humble act to draw near the table He has set for us; to receive Christ's body and blood in the appearance of the holy bread and wine, which is meant to nourish us. This intimate act of receiving Jesus gives God access to the deepest wounds in our heart. By His own Word, when touching Jesus, He cannot help but heal us.

"But Jesus said, 'Someone touched me; I know that power has gone out from me.' Then the woman, seeing that she could not go unnoticed, came trembling and fell at his feet. In the presence of all the people, she told why she had touched him and how she had been instantly healed" (Luke 8:46–47, NIV).

*****

I can still feel the welcome chill that seeped through the dampened sundress I wore as I leaned my back against the cool tiles in the entrance of that little church, back in 1989. Welcoming a reprieve from the scorching sun and rising temperature outside, I waited as the rest of our group gathered in the dim vestibule. We had made our way through the streets of Santarem, Portugal, to arrive at Saint Stephen's, the Church of the Holy Miracle. We were on a pilgrimage visiting the apparition site in Fatima where Our Blessed Mother, the Virgin Mary, appeared to three shepherd children in 1917, and the church was a side trip. Our tour guide patiently waited to begin his story until the last of our large group of nearly fifty teenagers and adults stepped through the doors. Once assembled, he began sharing the incredible story.

The miracle we were about to observe took place in the thirteenth century when an unhappy woman sought out the advice of a known sorceress for help with her marital problems. The distraught woman was told the price for such service would be to obtain a stolen consecrated Host. Although knowing she would be committing a terrible sacrilege, the desperate woman agreed to the sorceress' condition. The next time the troubled woman attended Mass, she removed the Host from her mouth and wrapped it in her veil. Unknown to her, the Host began to bleed profusely as she left the church. On her way to the sorceress' house, a passerby pointed out that the woman was leaving a trail of blood. Quickly rushing home instead, she hid the bloody veil and Host in the bottom of a trunk.

Later that night, the sleeping couple was awakened by rays of mysterious bright light illuminating the entire room. After confessing her sin to her husband, they both prayed in adoration on their knees until morning. At dawn, they notified the priest and he returned the Holy Host to the church. To contain the blood, it was encased in beeswax and secured in the tabernacle. When the tabernacle was later opened, it was discovered that the wax that contained the Host was broken into pieces and the Precious Blood and Host were miraculously enclosed in a crystal Pyx. Nearly eight hundred years have since passed and the Precious Blood remains liquid, defying the natural laws of science. Periodically happening throughout time and worldwide, many Miraculous Hosts are now being substantiated by modern technology to be the living flesh and blood of the human heart. Part bread, part flesh, in keeping with our belief in transubstantiation, inseparable. Testing continues to reveal the changing Hosts as AB positive blood type and to be a recently, severely, tortured heart of a man born of the Middle East.

After relating the miraculous story, our guide led us in solemn silence up the aisle toward the altar. We were about to behold the miracle. I sank with relief onto the worn, wooden pew near the front of the church. At the time, I was pregnant with my third child, and my legs ached from all the walking that day. I lifted my swollen feet, one at a time, resting them on the narrow kneeler. The afternoon sun filtered softly in through the windows. I thought if I closed my eyes for even a moment I would be fast asleep.

A chiming bell soon echoed through the cavernous nave of the church causing me to rise to my feet with the others. The priest approached the altar carrying the Miraculous Host displayed in a Monstrance. The wide band of cloth draped over his shoulders concealed his bare hands in its folds preventing him from directly touching the Monstrance. My heart began to pound, and I felt a burning heat, deep within my chest. All my complaints vanished and sinking to my knees, one thought filled my mind, "My Lord and my God!"

I began to wonder at my response. What was happening? I was a cradle Catholic, a believer since birth. I had twelve years of Catholic school education. I had a conversion of heart and had returned to minister to the youth in my parish. I had experienced Life in the Spirit. Yet now the Spirit in me spoke of its own accord, a witness to God's Presence before me in the Eucharist that I had so nonchalantly consumed for most of my life. How had I somehow missed what was gifted to me since I was seven years old; the Real Presence—body, blood, soul and divinity of Jesus Christ offered and received in the Holy Eucharist, every day, every hour, around the world.

"Then the Jews began to argue sharply among themselves, 'How can this man give us his flesh to eat?' Jesus said to them, 'Very truly I tell you, unless you eat the flesh of the Son of Man and drink His blood you have no life in you. Whoever eats my flesh and drinks my blood has eternal life, and I will raise them up at the last day. For my flesh is real food and my blood is real drink. Whoever eats my flesh and drinks my blood remains in me, and I in them.'" (John 6:52–56, NIV)

A joy so sweet that it brought tears to my eyes was followed by a stinging remorse as I realized the ramifications of the revelation. I no longer saw the Catholic Church as an institution of rules and regulations limiting freedom or choice, but as the caretaker through time, since Jesus's death and resurrection, of the Mystery of His Real Presence on earth.

When the priest indicated we were welcome to come forward so each of us could venerate the Holy Miracle, I braced myself not knowing what to expect. As I approached the altar, I became awed by God's Presence. When Father offered the Pyx to be kissed, I was torn between wanting to loudly exclaim, "I am Yours!" falling prostrate on the ground and running the other way, in a feeble attempt to try to hide my selfish soul. So I simply lowered my head and received the touch of the Monstrance on my forehead, receiving all that He so lovingly chose to give.

"And without faith it is impossible to please Him, for he who comes to God must believe that He is and that He is a rewarder of those who seek Him" (Heb. 11:6, NASB).

Twenty-five years have passed since the Lord revealed His true presence to me in the little church in Santarem. Now, as I sit in front of the Eucharist during my hour of adoration, I hand over the petitions filling my mind and lay down the restlessness in my soul until I become completely still. Little by little, I begin to see an inner vision. I see the same meadow where I rested in my healing prayer many times before. Frequently in my meditations, I would wind up at the knee of the Good Shepherd, looking like a small child. Golden haired and beautiful, my likeness reflecting how I longed to appear, how I imagined He wanted me to be.

> "Father, I desire that they also, whom You have given Me, *be with Me where I am*, so that they may see My glory which You have given Me, for You loved Me before the foundation of the world" (John 17:24, NASB).

This time though, I do not see the image that had given me delight in the past when Jesus was restoring my wounded soul. Instead I see myself, the straggly tawny-haired, cross-eyed, round-bellied child wearing the worn cast-off gown she had found discarded on the floor of her sisters' closet. Tears of love and gratitude fill my eyes as I look up into the serene face of Jesus, my Lord and my Savior. Joy radiates from His countenance, His piercing eyes revealing the Truth, "*I Love You.*" Suddenly, I am beautiful and precious because He made me . . . just as *I am*.

"I will not leave you as orphans; I will
come to you" (John 14:18, NIV).

Jesus is alive! We are never too far for Him to reach
us, and we are never too wounded to reach out to help
others. He lives and breathes and moves on earth in believers, in the Body of Christ. At times, we may hesitate to
move or speak up when we feel the nudge to share what
God is doing and saying to us. Perhaps we may think the
Holy Spirit's call is really our own imaginings. Yet consider,
our story may contain the key to unlock another's prison.
When God observes the brokenhearted, the ill and suffering, the downcast and outcast through our eyes, He equips
us to reach out and help. Would it make any difference if
we did? The answer is *yes*!

"Very truly I tell you, whoever believes
in me will do the works I have been doing,
and they will do even greater things than
these, because I am going to the Father"
(John 14–12, NIV).

The world is yearning for the Savior. If looking for
Jesus, you will find Him in His Word, in the hearts of His
people, and in a very real way waiting in all the tabernacles
of the world. *Come*, first let us adore Him! How many sig-
nificant encounters and signs of Christ's presence are missed
because our ears are tuned into our rational mind and not
to our hearts where He speaks. We hear more clearly when
we sit quietly in His presence. Will God's promise *to be*

with us, protect us, and *give us the words to say when we need them,* be enough for us to believe and step out in faith?

> "Then I heard a loud voice saying in heaven, 'Now salvation, and strength, and the kingdom of our God, and the power of His Christ have come, for the accuser of our brethren, who accused them before our God day and night, has been cast down. And they overcame him by the blood of the Lamb and by the word of their testimony, and they did not love their lives to the death.'" (Rev. 12:10–11, NKJV)

Each moment spent in prayer and worship contains heaven's currency, in exchange flow God's blessing, healing, and peace. We possess a solid foundation of God's Truth when we know His Word in the Holy Scriptures. It will hold us up, so we will not crumble when our adversary strikes. Every word of our story is imbued with purpose. God is doing something beautiful to behold with your story. Do not hesitate to give Jesus complete access to your heart, and He will change the way you view your world. Though you may feel at times you have evidence to the contrary, *He was and is and always will be* with you, every step of the way. Do not miss Christ's presence in your life. If you look closely, you too will find He has written a *Message of Love* in your story, and longs that you share it with the world around you.

"Do not let this Book of the Law depart from your mouth; meditate on it day and night, so that you may be careful to do everything written in it. Then you will be prosperous and successful. Have I not commanded you? Be strong and courageous. Do not be terrified; do not be discouraged, for the LORD your God will be with you wherever you go" (Joshua 1:8–9, NASB).

JESUS, I TRUST YOU

"I shall not die, but live, and
declare the works of the LORD"
(Ps. 118:17, KJV).

"And they overcame him because of the blood of the Lamb and because of the word of their testimony, and they did not love their life even when faced with death." Revelation 12:11

Resources

www.mustardseed.live
www.albrecht1.juiceplus.com
www.wholefoodsforkids.com
www.hempworx.com/ealbrecht
www.transformationprayer.org
www.leberwellness.com
www.rfsafe.com
www.nhsofarizona.com/w-lee-cowden-md
www.truefocushealth.com
www.cancer.gov
www.ihcenter.net
www.crunchi.com/healthpeak
www.truerife.com

ABOUT THE AUTHOR

Born into a large Catholic family, Eileen returned to her faith after a tumultuous youth to become involved as a songwriter and youth group music minister in her church. She is a speaker at health lectures and conferences, moms' groups, schools, community classes, and bible studies, inspiring many to become sensitive to the Holy Spirit's directives, courageously take action, and become proactive in protecting their family's health.

In the face of tragedy and illness, this family's collective faith grows stronger and is heroically passed down the family line. As a single mother of four children, Eileen faced horrific challenges in seeking help for her son who at three years old was diagnosed with leukemia, and by age seven, after suffering chemotherapy and radiation, a bone marrow transplant that resulted in a secondary cancer, was given up for lost. She then found herself choosing to stand on the Word of God, facing and making some of the most difficult decisions that a mother can be asked to make, with the strength of generations of faith to guide her.

Eileen has twenty-four years of experience as a licensed childcare provider. Along with her husband David Albrecht,

ND, her mission now is to bring mothers together to share their struggles and support one another on their journey to better health. Eileen's powerful mustard seed of faith continues through the years to testify to the healing that happens when trusting in the Father's unfailing love.

*If you have faith as small as a mustard
seed, you can say to this mountain,
'Move from here to there,' and it will move.
Nothing will be impossible for you.*
(Matthew 17:20 NIV)

——— ——— ——— ——— ——— ——— ——— ——— ——— ———

*"May the LORD, the God of your ancestors, increase you
a thousand times and bless you as He has promised!"*
(Deuteronomy 1:11 NIV)

——— ——— ——— ——— ——— ——— ——— ——— ——— ———

*He shall not fear an ill report; his heart is
steadfast trusting in the Lord.*
(Psalm 112:7 NABRE)

——— ——— ——— ——— ——— ——— ——— ——— ——— ———

*Say to the fearful of heart: Be strong, do not fear!
Here is your God, He comes with vindication;
With divine recompense He comes to save you.*
(Isaiah 35:4 NABRE)

——— ——— ——— ——— ——— ——— ——— ——— ——— ———

So, if the Son sets you free, you will be free indeed.
(John 8:36 NIV)

——— ——— ——— ——— ——— ——— ——— ——— ——— ———

A new heart also will I give you, and a
new spirit will I put within you:
and I will take away the stony heart out of your flesh,
and I will give you a heart of flesh.
(Ezekiel 36:26 KJV)

— — — — — — — — — — — — — — — — — —

Send out your light and your truth;
let them lead me; let them
bring me to your holy hill and to your dwelling!
(Psalm 43:3 ESV)

— — — — — — — — — — — — — — — — — —

So, will My word be which goes forth from My mouth;
It will not return to Me empty, without accomplishing
what I desire, and without succeeding in the
matter for which I sent it.
(Isaiah 55:11 NASB)

— — — — — — — — — — — — — — — — — —

And He has said to me, 'My grace is
sufficient for you, for power is
perfected in weakness.' Most gladly, therefore, I will rather
boast about my weaknesses, so that the
power of Christ may dwell in me.
(2 Corinthians 12:9 NASB)

— — — — — — — — — — — — — — — — — —

Now to Him who is able to do far more
abundantly beyond all that
we ask or think, according to the power that works within us.
(Ephesians 3:20 NASB)

The thief comes only to steal and kill and destroy.
I came that they may have life and have it abundantly.
(John 10:10 ESV)

He set forth before them, saying,
'The Kingdom of heaven is like a grain of Mustard Seed,
which a man took and sowed in his
field. Of all the seeds it is the
smallest, but when it has grown it is
the largest of the garden herbs
and becomes a tree, so that the birds of the air come
and find shelter in its branches.'
(Matthew 13:31-32 ESV)

Let us then with confidence draw near
to the throne of grace, that we
may receive mercy and find grace to help in time of need.
(Hebrews 4:16 ESV)

For He will give His angels charge concerning you, to guard you in all your ways. They will bear you up in their hands, that you do not strike your foot against a stone.
(Psalm 91:11-12 NIV)

---

*Before I formed you in the womb I knew
you before you were born,
I set you apart; I appointed you as a prophet to the nations.*
(Jeremiah 1:5 NIV)

---

*He has made everything beautiful in its
time. He has also set eternity
in the hearts of men; yet they cannot fathom what God has
done from beginning to end.*
(Ecclesiastes 3:11 NIV)

---

*For it was you who formed my inward parts; you knit
me together in my mother's womb. I praise you, for I am
fearfully and wonderfully made. Wonderful are your works;
that I know very well. My frame was not hidden from
you, when I was being made in secret, intricately woven
in the depths of the earth. Your eyes beheld my unformed
substance. In your book were written all the days that
were formed for me, when none of them as yet existed*
(Psalm 139: 13 ESV).

For just as the sufferings of Christ are ours in abundance
so also, our comfort is abundant through Christ.
(2 Corinthians 1:5 NASB)

I am crucified with Christ; and it is no longer I who live,
but it is Christ who lives in me.
(Galatians 2:20 NIV)

Consider it all joy, my brothers, when you encounter
various trials, for you know that the testing of your faith
produces perseverance. And let perseverance be perfect, so
that you may be perfect and complete, lacking in nothing.
(James 1:2-4 NABRE)

Two are better than one, because they have a good reward
for their toil. For if they fall, one will lift up his fellow.
But woe to him who is alone when he falls
and has not another to lift him up!
(Ecclesiastes 4:9-12 ESV)

And we know that God causes all things
to work together for good to those
who love God, to those who are called
according to His purpose.

(Romans 8:28 NASB)

Come to me, all who labor and are heavy laden,
and I will give you rest. Take my yoke
upon you, and learn from me, for I am
gentle and lowly in heart, and you
will find rest for your souls. For my yoke
is easy, and my burden is light.
(Matthew 11:28-30 ESV)

But thanks be to God! He gives us the victory
through our Lord Jesus Christ.
(1 Corinthians 15:57 NIV)

I will give them a heart to know Me, for I am the Lord;
and they will be My people, and I will be their God,
for they will return to Me with their whole heart.
(Jeremiah 24:7 NIV)

Now faith is the assurance of things hoped for,
the conviction of things not seen.
(Hebrews 11:1 NIV)

When Jesus saw his mother there, and the disciple whom he loved standing nearby, he said to her, 'Woman, here is your son,' and to the disciple, 'Here is your mother.' From that time on, this disciple took her into his home (John 19:26-27 NIV).

Therefore, I tell you, do not worry about your life, what you will eat or drink, or about your body, what you will wear. Isn't there more to life than food and more to the body than clothing? Look at the birds in the sky: They do not sow, or reap, or gather into barns, yet your heavenly Father feeds them. Are you not of more value than they? (Matthew 6:25-26 ESV).

The LORD appeared to him from afar, saying, 'I have loved you with an everlasting love; Therefore, I have drawn you with loving kindness.' (Jeremiah 31:3 NASB)

But the Helper, the Holy Spirit, whom the Father will send in my name, he will teach you all things and bring to your remembrance all that I have said to you. (John 14:26 NASB)

---

*You did not choose Me but I chose you, and appointed
you that you would go and bear fruit, and that
your fruit would remain, so that whatever you ask
of the Father in My Name He may give to you*
(John 15:16 NASB).

---

*The Lord is my light and my salvation;
whom shall I fear? The Lord
is the stronghold of my life; of whom shall I be afraid?*
(Psalm 27:1 NIV)

---

*First of all, then, I urge that supplications,
prayers, intercessions,
and thanksgivings be made for all people*
(1 Timothy 2 NIV).

---

*Do not be anxious about anything, but in everything
by prayer and supplication with thanksgiving let your
requests be made known to God. And the peace of
God, which surpasses all understanding, will guard
your hearts and your minds in Christ Jesus*
(Philippians 4:6-7 NIV).

Do not be afraid, for I am with you. Don't be discouraged,
for I am your God. I will strengthen you and help you.
I will hold you up with my victorious right hand.
(Isaiah 41:10 NLT)

— — — — — — — — — — — — — — — —

Though He slay me, yet will I trust Him. Even so,
I will defend my own ways before Him.
(Job 13:15 NKJV)

— — — — — — — — — — — — — — — —

Let us then with confidence draw near
to the throne of grace that we
may receive mercy and find grace to help in time of need.
(Hebrews 4:16 ESV)

— — — — — — — — — — — — — — — —

But when Jesus heard it, he answered him, saying, 'Fear not:
believe only, and she shall be made whole.'
(Luke 8:50 KJV)

— — — — — — — — — — — — — — — —

Fear is useless, what is needed is TRUST.
(Mark 5: 36 TLB)

— — — — — — — — — — — — — — — —

*Beloved, do not be surprised at the fiery ordeal
among you, which comes upon you for your testing,
as though some strange thing were happening to
you; but to the degree that you share the sufferings of
Christ, keep on rejoicing, so that also at the revelation
of His glory you may rejoice with exultation*
(1 Peter 4:12-13 NASB).

---

*And these signs will accompany those who believe: in my
name they will cast out demons; they will speak in new
tongues; they will pick up serpents with their hands; and
if they drink any deadly poison, it will not hurt them; they
will lay their hands on the sick, and they will recover*
(Mark 16: 17-18 NIV).

---

*Keep these words that I am commanding you today in your
heart. Recite them to your children and talk about them
when you are at home and when you are away, when you
lie down and when you rise. Bind them as a sign on your
hand, fix them as an emblem on your forehead, and write
them on the doorposts of your house and on your gates*
(Deuteronomy 6:6 NIV).

For we wrestle not against flesh and blood, but against principalities, against powers, against the rulers of the darkness of this world, against spiritual wickedness in high places
(Ephesians 6:12 KJV).

With every prayer and petition, pray at all times in the Spirit, and to this end be alert, with all perseverance and requests for all the saints.
(Ephesians 6:18 NET)

But, as it is written, 'What no eye has seen, nor ear heard, nor the heart of man imagined, what God has prepared for those who love him.'
(1 Corinthians 2:9 NABRE)

Beloved, I pray that all may go well with you and that you may be in good health, even as your soul prospers.
(3 John 1:2 ESV)

Rejoice always, pray without ceasing,
give thanks in all circumstances;
for this is the will of God in Christ Jesus for you.
(1 Thessalonians 5:16-18 ESV)

But do not ignore this one fact, beloved, that with the
Lord one day is like a thousand years[b] and 2121
a thousand years like one day. 9 The Lord does not
delay his promise, as some regard "delay," but he is
2122 patient with you, not wishing that any should
perish but that all should come to repentance
(2 (Peter 3:8 NABRE).

Love the Lord your God with all your heart,
with all your soul, and with all your mind.
(Luke 10:27 NIV)

By this everyone will know that you are my disciples,
if you love one another.
(John 13:35 NIV)

By this everyone will know that you are my disciples,
if you love one another.
(John 13:35 ESV)

Love is patient, love is kind. It does not envy, it does not
boast, it is not proud. It is not rude, it is not self-seeking,
it is not easily angered, it keeps no record of wrongs. Love
does not delight in evil but rejoices with the truth. It always
protects, always trusts, always hopes, always perseveres
(1 Corinthians 13:4 NIV).

O, Lord my God, I cried out to you
and you healed me.
(Psalm 30:3 NKJV)

My sheep hear My voice, and I know
them, and they follow Me.
(John 10:27 NKJV)

---

*These things I have spoken to you, so that in Me you
may have peace. In the world you will have tribulation
but take courage; I have overcome the world*
(John 16:33 NKJV).

---

*But it is the spirit in a man, the breath of the Almighty that
gives him understanding. It is not only the old who are wise,
not only the aged who understand what is right. Therefore,
I say: 'Listen to me; I too will tell you what I know'*
(Job 32:8 NASB).

---

*I keep asking that the God of our Lord
Jesus Christ, the glorious
Father, may give you the Spirit of wisdom and revelation,
so that you may know Him better.*
(Ephesians 1:17 NIV).

---

*Before I was afflicted I went astray,
but now I obey your word.
You are good and what you do is good, teach me your decrees.*
(Psalm 119:67-68 NIV)

Finally, brethren, whatsoever things are true, whatsoever
things are honest, whatsoever things are just, whatsoever
things are pure, whatsoever things are lovely, whatsoever
things are of good report; if there be any virtue, and
if there be any praise, think on these things
(Philippians 4:8 KJV).

- - - - - - - - - - - - - - - - -

By your endurance you will gain your lives.
(Luke 21:19 NASB)

- - - - - - - - - - - - - - - - -

Even when we are too weak to have any
faith left, He remains faithful
to us. And He will always carry out his promises to us.
(Timothy 2:13 TLB)

- - - - - - - - - - - - - - - - -

He will be like a tree planted by the water that sends
out its roots by the stream. It does not fear when heat
comes; its leaves are always green. It has no worries
in a year of drought and never fails to bear fruit
(Jeremiah 17:8 ESV).

- - - - - - - - - - - - - - - - -

Come and see what God has done,
His awesome deeds for us!
(Psalm 66:5 NIV)

— — — — — — — — — — — — — —

For since in the wisdom of God, the world through its wisdom
did not know Him, God was pleased through the foolishness
of what was preached to save those who believe.
(Corinthians1:21 NIV)

— — — — — — — — — — — — — —

And when they drink deadly poison,
it will not hurt them at all;
they will place their hands on sick
people and they will get well.
(Mark 16:18 NIV)

— — — — — — — — — — — — — —

I can do all things through Christ who strengthens me.
(Philippians 4:13 NIV)

— — — — — — — — — — — — — —

For no word from God will ever fail.
(Luke 1:37 NIV)

— — — — — — — — — — — — — —

*Be alert and of sober mind. Your enemy
the devil prowls around
like a roaring lion looking for someone to devour.*
(Peter 1 5:8 NIV)

---

*The light shines in the darkness, and the
darkness has not overcome it.*
(John 1:5 NIV)

---

*I will bless the Lord at all times; His praise shall continually
be in my mouth. My soul will glory in the Lord; let the
humble hear and be glad. Oh, magnify the Lord with
me, and let us exalt his name together! I sought the Lord,
and he answered me and delivered me from all my fears*
(Psalm 34:1-4 NABRE).

---

*My flesh and my heart may fail, But God is the rock
and strength of my heart and my portion forever.*
(Psalm 73:26 NIV)

In my distress, I called out: Lord! I cried out to my God.
From His Temple He heard my voice. My cry to Him reached
His ears. He parted the heavens and came down, a dark
cloud under His feet. The Lord thundered from heaven, the
Most High made His voice resound. He let fly His arrows
and scattered them, shot His lightning bolts and dispersed
them. He reached down from on high and seized me. He set
me free in the open: He rescued me because He loves me!
(Psalm 18: 7-20 NIV)

For He will command His angels concerning you
to guard you in all of your ways.
(Psalm 91:11 NIV)

See that you do not despise one of these little ones.
For I tell you that in heaven their angels always
see the face of my Father who is in heaven.
(Matthew 18:10 NIV)

So we can say with confidence, "The Lord is my helper, so
I will have no fear. What can mere people do to me?
(Hebrews 13:6 NIV)

---

*We demolish arguments and every
pretension that sets itself up against
the knowledge of God, and we take captive every thought
to make it obedient to Christ.*
(2 Corinthians 10:5 NIV)

---

*In the same way, the Spirit helps us in our weakness.
We do not know what we ought to pray for, but the
Spirit himself intercedes for us with groans that words
cannot express. And he who searches our hearts knows
the mind of the Spirit, because the Spirit intercedes
for the saints in accordance with God's will*
(Romans 8:26-27 NIV).

---

*Be strong and bold; have no fear or dread of them, because
it is the Lord your God who goes with you; he
will not fail you or forsake you.*
(Deuteronomy 31:6 NKJV)

---

*For I am the LORD your God who takes hold of your right
hand and says to you, 'Do not fear; I will help you.'*
(Isaiah 41:13 NIV)

---

*Whenever the cloud was lifted from over the tent,
afterward the sons of Israel would then set out; and in
the place where the cloud settled down, there the sons
of Israel would camp. At the command of the LORD
the sons of Israel would set out, and at the command
of the LORD they would camp; as long as the cloud
settled over the tabernacle, they remained camped*
(Numbers 9:17-18 NASB).

---

*You keep track of all my sorrows. You
have collected all my tears in
your bottle. You have recorded each one
in your book* (Psalm 56:8 NLT).

---

*Behold, I have given you every plant yielding seed that
is on the surface of all the earth, and every tree which
has fruit yielding seed; it shall be food for you.*
(Genesis 1:29 NASB)

---

*So, do not be like them; for your Father knows
what you need before you ask Him.*
(Matthew 6:8 NIV)

At the end of the ten days they looked
healthier and better nourished
than any of the young men who ate the royal food.
(Daniel 1:15 NIV)

Each of you should use whatever gift you
have received to serve others,
as faithful stewards of God's grace in its various forms.
(1 Peter 4:10 NIV)

Or do you not know that your body is a
temple of the Holy Spirit who is
in you, whom you have from God, and
that you are not your own?
(1 Corinthians 6:19 NIV)

It is God who arms me with strength and makes my
way perfect. He makes my feet like the feet of a deer; he
enables me to stand on the heights. He trains my hands
for battle; my arms can bend a bow of bronze. You give
me your shield of victory, and your right hand sustains
me; you stoop down to make me great. You broaden
the path beneath me, so that my ankles do not turn.
(Psalm 18:32-36 NLT).

Great peace have those who love your law,
and nothing can make them stumble.
(Psalm 119:165 NIV)

'For I know the plans I have for you,'
declares the Lord, 'Plans to prosper
you and not to harm you, plans to give
you a hope and a future.'
(Jeremiah 29:11 NIV)

And behold, this day I am going the way of all the earth.
Know in all your hearts and in all your souls that not
one thing has failed of all the good things which the
Lord your God promised concerning you. All have come
to pass for you; not one thing of them has failed."
(Joshua 23:14 NKJV).

And without faith it is impossible to please
Him, for he who comes to God must
believe that He is and that He is a
rewarder of those who seek Him.
(Hebrews 11:6 NIV)

And all things, whatever you shall ask in prayer,
believing, you shall receive.
(Matthew 21: 22 KJV)

— — — — — — — — — — — — — — —

Remember how the Lord your God led you all the way
in the desert these forty years, to humble you and to test
you in order to know what was in your heart, whether or
not you would keep his commands. He humbled you . . .
to teach you that man does not live by bread alone but
on every word that comes from the mouth of the Lord
(Deuteronomy 8:2-3 ISV).

— — — — — — — — — — — — — — —

Trust in the LORD with all your heart, and
do not lean on your own understanding. In
all your ways acknowledge him, and
He will make straight your paths.
(Proverbs 3:5-6 ESV)

— — — — — — — — — — — — — — —

Even though I walk through the darkest valley; I fear no evil;
for you are with me; your rod and
your staff; they comfort me.
(Psalm 23:4 NIV)

— — — — — — — — — — — — — — —

*And he said to them, "This kind cannot be
driven out by anything but prayer."*
(Mark 9:29 NASB)

Do not be conformed to this world, but ***be
transformed by the renewing of
your mind,*** *so that you may prove what the will of God is,
that which is good and acceptable and perfect.*
(Romans 12:2 NASB)

---

*The Lord is my light and my salvation
– whom shall I fear? The Lord
is the stronghold of my life – of whom shall I be afraid?*
(Psalm 27:1 NIV)

---

*And He said to me, 'My grace is sufficient
for you, for My strength is made
perfect in weakness.' Therefore, most
gladly I will rather boast in
my infirmities, that the power of Christ may rest upon me.*
(Corinthians 12:9 NIV)

---

*Why, my soul, are you downcast? Why
so disturbed within me?
Put your hope in God, for I will yet praise him,
my Savior and my God.*
(Psalm 43:5 NIV)

---

*Therefore, put on the full armor of God, so that when the
day of evil comes, you may be able to stand your ground,
and after you have done everything, to stand.*
(Ephesians 6:13 NIV)

---

*In peace I will both lie down and sleep, For You
alone, O Lord, make me dwell in safety.*
(Psalm 4:8 ESV)

---

*When you go through deep waters and
great trouble, I will be with you.
When you go through rivers of difficulty, you will not drown!*
(Isaiah 43:2 NLV)

He said unto me, My grace is sufficient for thee;
for My strength is made perfect in weakness. Most
gladly therefore will I rather glory in my infirmities
that the power of Christ may rest upon me
(2 Corinthians 12:9 KJV).

Let us hold unswervingly to the hope we profess, for
He who promised is faithful. And let us consider how
we may spur one another on toward love and good
deeds, not giving up meeting together, as some are in
the habit of doing, but encouraging one another—
and all the more as you see the Day approaching
(Hebrews 10:23-25 NIV).

Praise the Lord, O my soul, and forget not all His
benefits – who forgives all your sins and heals all
your diseases, who redeems your life from the pit
and crowns you with love and compassion.
(Psalm 103:3-4 NIV).

But if any of you lacks wisdom, let him ask of God, who
gives to all generously and without reproach,
and it will be given to him.
(James 1:5 ESV).

But the wisdom that comes from heaven is first of all pure; then peace-loving, considerate, submissive, full of mercy and good fruit, impartial and sincere (James 3:17 NIV).

But seek ye first the kingdom of God, and his righteousness; and all these things shall be added unto you (Matthew 6:33 ESV).

But I have raised you up for this very purpose, that I might show you My power and that my Name might be proclaimed in all the earth. (Exodus 9:16 NIV)

In returning [to Me] and rest you shall be saved, in quietness and confident trust is your strength (Isaiah 30:15 KJV).

After you have suffered a little while, the God of all grace, who has called you to his eternal glory in Christ, will himself restore, confirm, strengthen, and establish you. (1 Peter 5:10 ESV).

I have told you these things, so that in me you may have peace. In this world you will have trouble. But take heart! I have overcome the world.
(John 16:33).

Ask and it will be given to you; seek and you will find; knock and the door will be opened to you.
(Matthew 7:7 NIV)

But when you ask, you must believe and not doubt, because the one who doubts is like a wave of the sea, blown and tossed by the wind
(James 1:6 NIV).

I have fought a good fight, I have finished my course, I have kept the faith: Henceforth there is laid up for me a crown of righteousness, which the Lord, the righteous judge, shall give me at that day: and not to me only, but unto all them also that have longed for his appearance
(2 Timothy 4:7-8 KJV).

Then the Lord said to Moses, 'Make a fiery serpent, and set it on a pole; and it shall be that everyone who is bitten, when he looks at it, shall live.' So Moses made a bronze serpent, and put it on a pole; and so it was, if a serpent had bitten anyone, when he looked at the bronze serpent, he lived.
(Numbers 21:4-9 ESV).

Then shall your light break forth like the dawn, and your healing shall spring up speedily; your righteousness shall go before you; the glory of the Lord shall be your rear guard
(Isaiah 58:8 ESV).

For the eyes of the LORD roam throughout the entire earth, to strengthen those whose heart is true to him.
(2 Chronicles 16:9a NIV)

And we all, who with unveiled faces contemplate the Lord's glory, are being transformed into His image with ever-increasing glory, which comes from the Lord, who is the Spirit.
(2 Corinthians 3:18 NIV).

When He had reclined at the table with them, He took the bread and blessed it, and breaking it, He began giving it to them. Then their eyes were opened and they recognized Him.
(Luke 24:30-31 NASB).

But Jesus said, 'Someone touched me; I know that power has gone out from me.' Then the woman, seeing that she could not go unnoticed, came trembling and fell at his feet. In the presence of all the people, she told why she had touched him and how she had been instantly healed
(Luke 8:46-47 NIV).

Then the Jews began to argue sharply among themselves, 'How can this man give us his flesh to eat?' Jesus said to them, 'Very truly I tell you, unless you eat the flesh of the Son of Man and drink His blood you have no life in you. Whoever eats my flesh and drinks my blood has eternal life, and I will raise them up at the last day. For my flesh is real food and my blood is real drink. Whoever eats my flesh and drinks my blood remains in me, and I in them'
(John 6:52-56 NIV).

And without faith it is impossible to please Him, for he who comes to God must believe that He is and that He is a rewarder of those who seek Him (Hebrews 11:6 NASB).

---

*Father, I desire that they also, whom You have given Me, **be with Me where I am,** so that they may see My glory which You have given Me, for You loved Me before the foundation of the world.* (John 17:24 NASB)

I will not leave you as orphans; I will come to you. (John 14:18 NIV)

Very truly I tell you, whoever believes in me will do the works I have been doing, and they will do even greater things than these, because I am going to the Father (John 14-12 NIV).

Then I heard a loud voice saying in heaven, 'Now salvation, and strength, and the kingdom of our God, and the power of His Christ have come, for the accuser of our brethren, who accused them before our God day and night, has been cast down. And they overcame him by the blood of the Lamb and by the word of their testimony, and they did not love their lives to the death'
(Revelation 12:10-11 NKJV).

"The Lord delights in those who fear Him, who put their hope in his unfailing love."
(Psalm 147:11 NIV)

"A wife of noble character who can find? She is worth far more than rubies. Her husband full confidence in her and lacks nothing of value"
(Prov. 39:10–11 NIV)

"For God so loved the world, that He gave His only Son, that whoever believes in Him should not 969 perish but have eternal life".
—John 3:16 (ESV)

"The spirit of the Lord God is upon me, because the Lord has anointed me; He has sent me to bring good news to the afflicted to bind up the brokenhearted, to proclaim liberty to the captives, release to the prisoners, to announce a year of favor from the Lord and a day of vindication by our God; to comfort all who mourn."
(Isa. 61:1–2, NABRE)

"Blessed are those who mourn, for they will be comforted"
(Matt. 5:4, NIV)

"Then the peace of God that surpasses all understanding will guard your hearts and minds in Christ."
(Phil 4:7, NABRE)

"Rejoice in hope, be patient in tribulation, be constant in prayer"
(Rom.12:12, ESV)

"Therefore, put on the full armor of God, so that when the day of evil comes, you may be able to stand your ground, and after you have done everything, to stand. Stand firm then, with the belt of truth buckled around your waist, with the breastplate of righteousness in place, and with your feet fitted with the readiness that comes from the gospel of peace. In addition to all this, take up the shield of faith, with which you can extinguish all the flaming arrows of the evil one. Take the helmet of salvation and the sword of the Spirit, which is the word of God."
(Eph. 6:13–17, NIV)

- — - — - — - — - — - — - — - — - — - — - — -

"The Lord, your God, is in your midst, a Mighty Savior. He will take great delight in you, He will quiet you with his love, He will rejoice over you with singing"
(Zep. 3:17, NIV)

- — - — - — - — - — - — - — - — - — - — -

I abandon myself to you O Lord, my God, my Savior and my King, and to your Mercy, to the intervention of the Most Holy Spirit, and to the intercession of Your Most Blessed Mother Mary, and to the prayers and the intentions of all your Saints and Angels in Heaven, for the redemption of souls. Amen.
(Eileen's prayer)

- — - — - — - — - — - — - — - — - — - — - — -

JESUS, I TRUST YOU

9 781644 167489